Understanding the Abortion Arguments

A Layperson's Guide

Dave Evans

Grosvenor House
Publishing Limited

This book is published by
Grosvenor House Publishing Ltd
Link House
140 The Broadway, Tolworth, Surrey, KT6 7HT.
www.grosvenorhousepublishing.co.uk

A CIP record for this book
is available from the British Library

ISBN 978-1-83975-937-6

Preface

Men never do evil so completely and cheerfully as when they do it from religious conviction. *–Blaise Pascal (1623–62), French mathematician, physicist, and philosopher.*

Those who can make you believe absurdities, can make you commit atrocities. *– Voltaire (1694–1778) French philosopher and writer.*

On 29 July 1994, Paul Jennings Hill (1954–2003), a former Presbyterian minister, shot and killed Dr John Bayard Britton, and his bodyguard, as they drove into a Pensacola abortion clinic. Following the shootings, Hill reportedly laid his shotgun on the ground and waited to be arrested. Executed by lethal injection on 3 September 2003 his final words were:

> The last thing I want to say: If you *believe* abortion is a lethal force, you should oppose the force and do what you have to do to stop it. May God help you to protect the unborn as you would want to be protected.

The day before his execution, the unrepentant Hill told reporters that he was following God's instructions when he shot Britton, and that he was sure he would be rewarded in heaven for his actions. Hill was not the first person to murder a doctor who performed abortions[1],

---

[1] Michael Griffin murdered Dr David Gunn on 10 March 1993 at the Pensacola Women's Medical Services clinic.

and neither was he the last[2], but this incident clearly shows that misguided religious conviction can compel individuals to carry out the most heinous of acts in the name of God.

Although the majority of anti-abortion violence, including assault and battery, bombings, arson, and acid attacks, have occurred in the United States, there have also been incidents recorded in Australia, Canada and New Zealand. Even in the United Kingdom, Christian anti-abortion groups are now becoming much more active, necessitating so-called buffer zones to be placed around some abortion clinics.

Those actions that are clearly against the law are condemned by most right-thinking individuals and need not be addressed here. However, there is a more insidious technique anti-abortionist are employing that this book sets out to refute.

Consider the following points raised in a leaflet, published in 2020[3], by a pressure group promoting a fundamentalist Christian viewpoint:

■ Abortion is significantly associated with an increased risk of breast cancer – by as much as

---

[2] Scott Roeder murdered Dr George Tiller on 31 May 2009, as he was serving as an usher in the foyer of a church in Wichita, Kansas. Additionally, a National Abortion Federation (NAF) 2018 Report, records 11 murders of clinical workers between 1990 and 2018.

[3] Taken from The Christian Institute's March 2020 leaflet entitled *Abortion*. I have chosen this leaflet, not because I am picking on any one religious' group, but because it is relatively recent, available for download and contains medical, religious and ethical statements with which I take issue.

44% after one abortion and even higher as the number increases.

- Women who have had an abortion experience an 81% higher risk of mental health problems when compared with women who have not had an abortion.

Notice, that these points have nothing whatsoever to do with whether abortion is unethical. They appear to be included in the leaflet simply to try and scare women away from procuring one. I take up the medical risks of abortion in Chapter 1, but for now just take note of the following statement on the National Health Service (NHS) website[4]:

> Having an abortion does not increase the risk of breast cancer or mental health issues.

When it comes to the actual morality of abortion, the leaflet makes the following points:

- The Bible is clear that abortion amounts to the taking of a life.
- The early Church "with unwavering consistency and with the strongest emphasis denounced the practice [of abortion]... not simply as inhuman, but as definitely murder"

However, look for the term *abortion* in the Bible and you will not find it! Although the leaflet does not explain what it means by the "early Church," no New

---

[4] www.nhs.uk/conditions/abortion/risks/ retrieved 10 February 2021.

Testament writer mentions abortion, and some prominent Christian saints, for example St Jerome, St Augustine and St Anselm, did not regard abortion in the early stages of pregnancy as murder! I consider the role the Bible plays in the abortion debate in Chapter 2. In Chapters 3 and 4 I consider the two different views that some Christians have taken when opposing abortion throughout their history.

For now though, just consider the following quotes from the 2014 report of the Department of Economic and Social Affairs of the United Nations (DESA), entitled *Abortion Polices and Reproductive Health around the World*:

> In 2013, **97 per cent of Governments permitted abortion to save a woman's life.** ... Chile, the Dominican Republic, El Salvador, the Holy See, Malta and Nicaragua did not permit abortion under any circumstances. *Page 3.*

> The proportion of countries permitting abortion for economic or social reasons or upon request also rose gradually between 1996 and 2013. In 2013, slightly over one third (36 per cent) of Governments permitted abortion for economic or social reasons, up from 31 per cent in 1996, **while 30 per cent of Governments allowed abortion upon request, up from 24 per cent in 1996.** *Page 6.*

> *Note: All emphasised text in* **bold**
> *is my doing unless otherwise stated.*

So, with 97% of countries permitting abortion to save a woman's life and 30% permitting it on request, it follows that the *belief* that abortion is **murder**[5] evidently is not one held by the lawmakers of these countries! In fact, as "murder" is a legal term, it follows that any abortion carried out under state-sanctioned procedures cannot be murder, and those claiming that it is are quite simply wrong!

Now, whilst some Christian groups wrongly claim that abortion is murder, and do their best to have them outlawed, the following **Key facts**[6], from the World Health Organization (WHO) show what happens when women cannot access safe abortion facilities:

> Each year between 4.7% – 13.2% of **maternal deaths can be attributed to unsafe** abortion (3).
>
> Around 7 million women are admitted to hospitals every year in developing countries, as a result of unsafe abortion (4).
>
> Almost every abortion death and disability could be prevented through sexuality education, use of effective contraception, **provision of safe, legal induced abortion,** and timely care for complications. (6)

And in their document *Safe abortion: technical and policy guidance for health systems*[7], they have the following:

> Over the past two decades, the health evidence, technologies and human rights rationale for providing

---

[5] The precise definition of murder varies from jurisdiction to jurisdiction, but for our purposes we can define it as *the **unlawful** killing of another human being without justification.*

[6] https://www.who.int/news-room/fact-sheets/detail/preventing-unsafe-abortion, retrieved 9 February 2020.

[7] Second edition published in 2012.

safe, comprehensive abortion care have evolved greatly. Despite these advances, an estimated 22 million abortions continue to be performed unsafely each year, **resulting in the death of an estimated 47 000 women and disabilities for an additional 5 million women** (1). *Page 1.*

Specifically, relevant for us, the report also includes the following:

Legal restrictions on abortion do not result in fewer abortions nor do they result in significant increases in birth rates (21, 22). Conversely, **laws and policies that facilitate access to safe abortion do not increase the rate or number of abortions.** The principle effect is to shift previously clandestine, unsafe procedures to legal and safe ones (21, 23). **Restricting legal access to abortion does not decrease the need for abortion, but it is likely to increase the number of women seeking illegal and unsafe abortions, leading to increased morbidity and mortality.** Legal restrictions also lead many women to seek services in other countries/states (24, 25), which is costly, delays access and creates social inequities. Restricting abortion, with the intent of boosting population has been well documented in several countries. In each case, abortion restrictions resulted in an increase of illegal and unsafe abortions and pregnancy-related mortality, with insignificant net increase in the population (26–29). *Page 90.*

So, if legal restrictions on abortion do not result in fewer abortions, whilst laws and policies that facilitate access to safe abortion do not increase the rate or number of abortions, it follows that campaigning for tighter legal restrictions on abortion risks putting more vulnerable women in danger of death or serious harm, for no apparent gain! I examine the morality of abortion in Chapter 5 and the legal considerations in Chapter 6.

The following Introduction contains some preliminary information intended to help readers unfamiliar with some of the topics covered later in this book.

Introduction

All men have opinions, but few men think. *Bishop Berkeley (1685–1753) Anglican bishop, philosopher and scientist.*

The greatest obstacle to progress is not the absence of knowledge but the illusion of knowledge. *Daniel J. Boorstin (1914–2004), American Social Historian.*

By the time any human being has reached adulthood, they will have acquired many **beliefs,** some of which may be sincerely and passionately held; to the point where those holding such beliefs are willing to both kill and be killed in order to defend.

Now, a belief is just something we assent to; an opinion we hold on a given topic. For example, many Christians in the past, relying on passages in their Bible, believed that the Earth was flat[8], rested on pillars[9], and was motionless with the Sun, Moon and stars circling around it[10]. However, today most Christians, although sadly not all, accept the fact that the Earth is not flat, does not rest on pillars and is revolving around our Sun, which is at the centre of our solar system. So, the important thing to bear in mind regarding **beliefs** is that

---

[8] See, for example, Isaiah 24:1, Daniel 4:10-11, Matthew 4:8 and Luke 4:5.

[9] See, for example, 1 Samuel 2:8, Job 9:6 and Psalms 75:3.

[10] See, for example, 1 Chronicles 16:30, Psalms 93:1, Psalms 96:10, Psalms 104:5 and Joshua 10:12.

no matter how sincerely and passionately they may be held, they could be wrong!

As the above illustrates, we should not uncritically believe what *authorities* want us to, as they can be wrong as well. Also, note that **knowledge** of our solar system developed *in spite* of religious scriptures and is *contrary* to them.

Nevertheless, we are all free to hold whatever beliefs we like, however ill-informed, providing they do not adversely impinge on other people. If they do, then we all have a **moral responsibility** to, at least, do everything we can to ensure that our **beliefs** are valid.

For example, in the Preface I mentioned that some Christians viewed abortion as "definitely murder" and are doing all they can to outlaw it, despite the very real danger that, if they succeed, it will result in much more maternal mortality and morbidity. However, many Christian groups recognize that legislation will not address the root of the problem and see abortion as a matter of individual conscience. For example, the 71st General Convention of the Episcopal Church, whilst opposing abortion as "a means of birth control, family planning, sex selection, or any reason of mere convenience," reaffirmed a resolution from the 69th General Convention, and includes the following[11]:

> We believe that legislation concerning abortions **will not address the root of the problem**. We therefore express **our deep conviction** that any proposed

---

[11] http://religiousinstitute.org/denom_statements/reaffirm-general-convention-statement-on-childbirth-and-abortion-0/

legislation on the part of national or state governments regarding abortions **must take special care to see that the individual conscience is respected**, and that **the responsibility of individuals to reach informed decisions in this matter is acknowledged and honored** as the position of this Church; and be it further

Resolved, That this 71st General Convention of the Episcopal Church express its unequivocal opposition to any legislative, executive or judicial action on the part of local, state or national governments that abridges the right of a woman to reach an informed decision about the termination of pregnancy or that would limit the access of a woman to safe means of acting on her decision.

So, clearly within Christianity itself there are diverse and even opposing views on the topic. The question is: Is there any way that we can make an informed, rational, and unbiased decision on the morality of abortion?

Well, we can all claim to **know** that 3 + 2 = 5 and, if in the unlikely event that anyone argues with us, we are **justified** in claiming that they are simply wrong, which is something easy to prove beyond doubt.

Unfortunately, there are very few things we can **know** with the same certainty as mathematical equations, and if someone disagrees with us on a particular issue, then we are left with the choice of either ignoring their point of view or examining the arguments they put forward to see if they are valid. The problem is that many people do not know how to examine arguments properly, or how to construct convincing arguments themselves.

All too often people, on different sides of an argument, simply gather some random pieces of information together and try to use them to **justify** the position that they have already adopted. Judging by the literature that I have seen, this is certainly the case when it comes to the topic of abortion. For example, anti-abortionists often claim that many women who have had abortions later come to regret it. Although this is probably true, it adds nothing to the question as to whether abortion is morally wrong, and laws need to be put in place to try and prevent it. Many women who have had an abortion are just as adamant that, for them, it was the right choice.

So, before moving on, I want to say a quick word about arguments in general. Especially when it comes to contentious arguments, they commonly involve a mixture of both **facts** and **values**, and what often drives the argument is differences in **values**. The relevant facts in a debate can generally be ascertained and agreed upon fairly quickly, but it is the relevant values that are the things we care about and what causes the disagreement.

So, one of the first things we need to do, in trying to understand the abortion argument, is to separate the relevant facts from the values involved in making a moral judgement on the matter. We can then use simple **logic** to examine the statements and claims from both sides.

Logic is an abstract system of rules, much like mathematics, that we can use to navigate from simple ideas to more complicated ideas without getting lost.

Simple logical statements take the form of **P therefore C**, where **P** represents the premise, or premises, we are using to derive **C**, our conclusion. **Therefore**, in the context of a **valid** logical statement means that, if you have **P** then you always (and I do mean always) get **C**. A commonly used example should make this clear:

P1. All men are mortal.
P2. Socrates is a man.
Therefore
C Socrates is mortal

Every argument can, and should, be broken down into simple logical statements, to see if the conclusion logically follows from the premises. However, all too often debates fail, and end up in *slanging matches*, because the two sides don't address these statements at all. Instead, they generate *tons* of new statements, trying to overwhelm their opponents with the sheer number of them.

Historically, it turns out that there have only ever been two reasons put forward to justify the claim that abortion is **morally** wrong, and these are referred to as the **perversity view** and the **ontological view**.

We will need to subject these two reasons to detailed logical analysis later, but put simply, the perversity view is the claim that abortion is a perversion of the true function of sex, which is solely (or at least primarily) for the purpose of procreation. In other words, if sex is only, or principally, for the purpose of bringing children into the world, then abortion thwarts this purpose and is, therefore, immoral.

The ontological view claims that the foetus is a human **person** and, as a human **person**, it should have the same rights afforded to it as any other human **person**, including the right to life. Therefore, abortion is immoral.

Because many Christians try to use passages from the Bible as *authoritative* statements endorsing their stance against abortion, before analysing both views, I want to examine these passages and put them in their original context.

However, because anti-abortionists use some, to say the least, very selective reports on the health issues concerning abortion, this will be the subject of my first chapter.

Chapter 1

The Medical Risks of Abortion

Nullius in verba (Take nobody's word for it) *Moto of the Royal Society*

Although the moto of the Royal Society may sound a tad cynical, it should act as a guard against uncritical acceptance of, so called, *facts* presented in leaflets espousing a specific point of view.

According to the Royal College of Obstetricians & Gynaecologists[12], breast cancer is the most common cancer in females, with a lifetime risk of one in nine in the UK and is the leading cause of death in women aged 35–54 years. Bearing this in mind, it is worth considering the effect that the following statement in the Christian Institute's leaflet, entitled *Abortion*, is likely to have on any woman considering having an abortion:

> It is widely recognised that carrying a first pregnancy to birth is protective against breast cancer.[15] However recent studies have also shown that abortion is **significantly associated** with an increased risk of breast cancer – **by as much as 44 per cent after one abortion and even higher as the number increases.**[16]

---

[12] From their *Pregnancy and Breast Cancer* Green-top Guideline No. 12, March 2011.

Clearly, if abortion was a causal risk factor for breast cancer, then it is something women should be aware of when considering having one. However, first notice the word **associated**. This does not mean **caused!** This becomes clear when we look at the actual studies 'Conclusion,' which states:

> **If IA were to be confirmed as a risk factor for breast cancer**, high rates of IA in China **may** contribute to increasing breast cancer rates.

IA refers to induced abortions as distinct from **SA**, which is spontaneous abortion, and the 'Conclusion' indicates that any possible causal link has yet to be confirmed. Why the reference to 'China' in the study? Well, the research only covers '14 provinces in China.' The Christian Institutes extract is taken from:

> Huang, Y, Zhang, X, Li, W et al, 'A meta-analysis of the association between induced abortion and breast cancer risk among Chinese females', *Cancer Causes Control*, 2014, 25, pages 227-236.

Cancer Causes & Control is an international journal of Studies of Cancer in the human population. As can be seen, the specific study is dated 2014. However, in 2015 the same journal published an article entitled *Association between abortion and breast cancer: an updated systematic review and meta-analysis based on prospective studies*, which has the following conclusion:

> In conclusion, the current prospective evidences **are not sufficient to support the positive association between abortion (including IA and SA) and breast cancer risk.**

However, we cannot simply draw rash conclusions that there is a null association between abortion and breast cancer risk based on current prospective evidences, and that there is no necessity to further conduct such studies.

Type "Abortion and Breast Cancer" into the Caner Research UK website[13] and you will find a report entitled *Pregnancies that end in miscarriage or abortion do not increase a woman's risk of developing breast cancer*. Although this study is dated 26 March 2004, it has the following:

> The research **included 44,000 breast cancer patients** who took part in studies where any history of abortion had been recorded before their cancer was diagnosed.
>
> The researchers compared the chances of developing breast cancer in women with and without any record of having had an abortion. This comparison gives the 'relative risk', **where a value of 1.0 or less means no adverse effect on the risk of developing breast cancer.** The relative risk of breast cancer for women who have had a miscarriage is 0.98. **For women who have had an induced abortion the relative risk of breast cancer is 0.93.**
>
> Professor Valerie Beral, Director of the Cancer Research UK's Epidemiology Unit at the University of Oxford, says: "This review of the worldwide evidence has shown that pregnancies that end in an abortion do not increase a woman's chances of developing breast cancer later in life."

---

[13] Last accessed 8 February 2021.

The American Cancer Society has the following on their website[14]:

Conclusion

The topic of abortion and breast cancer highlights many of the most challenging aspects of studies of people and how those studies do or do not translate into public health guidelines. The issue of abortion generates passionate viewpoints in many people. Breast cancer is the most common cancer in women aside from skin cancer; and breast cancer is the second leading cancer killer in women. **Still, the public is not well-served by false alarms.** At this time, **the scientific evidence does not support the notion that abortion of any kind raises the risk of breast cancer or any other type of cancer.**

And the National Health Service (NHS) website[15] confirms these findings:

Having an abortion does not increase the risk of **breast cancer** or **mental health issues.**

The NHS statement is interesting as it directly contradicts another statement found in the Christian Institute's leaflet regarding psychological risks. That is:

Over 98 per cent of abortions for residents of England and Wales in 2018 were carried out on the grounds

---

[14] https://www.cancer.org/cancer/cancer-causes/medical-treatments/abortion-and-breast-cancer-risk.html retrieved 9 February 2021.

[15] www.nhs.uk/conditions/abortion/risks/ retrieved 10 February 2021.

that 'continuing with the pregnancy would involve a greater risk to the woman's physical or mental health than having an abortion'.[20] **Yet women who have had an abortion experience an 81 per cent higher risk of mental health problems when compared with women who have not had an abortion.**[21]

The reference is to Coleman, P K, '*Abortion and mental health: quantitative synthesis and analysis of research published 1995-2009*, British Journal of Psychiatry, 199(3), 2011, pages 180-186. However, when we look at the actual article, we find:

> Women who had undergone an abortion experienced an 81% increased risk of mental health problems, **and nearly 10% of the incidence of mental health problems was shown to be attributable to abortion.**

It follows, therefore, that 71% (81% - 10%) of the increased risk of mental health problems was **not** shown to be attributable to abortion! Notice, though, that the Christian Institute's leaflet was not published until 2020, whereas Coleman's article appeared in 2011. Interestingly, published later that same year, we find another article, this time by the Academy of Medical Royal Colleges[16], entitled *Induced Abortion And Mental Health: A Systematic Review of the Mental Health Outcomes of Induced Abortion, Including their*

---

[16] The Academy of Medical Royal Colleges is the coordinating body for the UK and Ireland's 23 medical Royal Colleges and Faculties. Their role is to ensure that patients are safely and properly cared for by setting standards for the way doctors are educated, trained and monitored throughout their careers.

Prevalence and Associated Factors. The review was developed by the National Collaborating Centre for Mental Health (NCCMH)[17] and funded by the Department of Health. The *Executive Summary* contains the following:

Background

The majority of abortions carried out in the UK are done so on the grounds that continuing with the pregnancy would risk physical or psychological harm to the woman or child. However, there has been some concern in recent years that abortion itself may increase psychological risk and adversely affect the woman's mental health. **Opinion on this has varied, partly due to limitations in the research, different interpretations of the evidence and the ethical, religious and political issues surrounding abortion.** This report was commissioned **to review the best available evidence** on any association between induced abortion and mental health outcomes, and draw conclusions where possible.

In conjunction with other shortcomings mentioned in this article, regarding the Coleman review along with others, this article included:

In the Coleman review, outcomes for women who had had an abortion were compared with outcomes for women who had not had an abortion (no abortion,

---

[17] The NCCMH was established in 2001 at the Royal College of Psychiatrists, in partnership with the British Psychological Society. Its primary role is to develop evidence-based mental health reviews and clinical guidelines.

pregnancy delivered or unintended pregnancy delivered group). Details of the search strategy and the number of papers retrieved in the search were not provided, **nor was it clear why certain papers and outcomes were excluded from the review. ... Although studies were required to control for third variables, they were not required to control for mental health problems prior to the abortion.**

The second point is particularly relevant when we look at this report's findings:

Taking into account the broad range of studies and their limitations, the steering group concluded that, **on the best evidence available:**

- The rates of mental health problems for women with an unwanted pregnancy were the same whether they had an abortion or gave birth.
- An unwanted pregnancy was associated with an increased risk of mental health problems.
- The most reliable predictor of post-abortion mental health problems was having a history of mental health problems before the abortion.
- The factors associated with increased rates of mental health problems for women in the general population following birth and following abortion were similar.
- There were some additional factors associated with an increased risk of mental health problems specifically related to abortion, such as pressure from a partner to have an abortion and negative attitudes towards abortions in general and towards a woman's personal experience of the abortion.

The steering group also noted that:

- The rates of mental health problems after an abortion were higher when studies included women with previous mental health problems than in studies that excluded women with a history of mental health problems.
- A negative emotional reaction immediately following an abortion may be an indicator of poorer mental health outcomes.
- Meta-analyses in this area were of low quality, at significant risk of bias and offered no advantage over a rigorous systematic narrative review.
- Future practice and research should focus on the mental health needs associated with an unwanted pregnancy, rather than on the resolution of the pregnancy.

It is also worth noting the following:

Recommendations

In the light of these findings, it is important to consider the need **for support and care for all women who have an unwanted pregnancy** because the risk of mental health problems increases **whatever the pregnancy outcome.** If a woman has a negative attitude towards abortion, shows a negative emotional reaction to the abortion or is experiencing stressful life events, health and social care professionals should consider offering support, and where necessary treatment, because they are more likely than other women **who have an abortion** to develop mental health problems.

As well as the section entitled *SERIOUS CONSEQUENCES FOR THE MOTHER*, the Christian Institutes leaflet also has a section entitled *BABIES MAY*

FEEL PAIN AT 12 WEEKS, which includes the following:

> One of the biggest abortion providers in the UK, the British Pregnancy Advisory Service, argues that babies in the womb cannot feel pain before 28 weeks. Other groups say 24 weeks. **But both scientific research and medical practice utterly contradict the claim that unborn babies don't feel pain before these gestations. ...**
>
> In February 2018, the Government admitted that in-womb surgery – routinely available on the NHS – includes pain relief for the baby. Responding to a parliamentary question on spina bifida surgery, a health minister said: "Pain relief for the unborn baby will be delivered intra-operatively." She added: "The surgery takes place between 20 and 26 weeks of gestation."[13] **So even in Parliament the need for pain relief is recognised from 20 weeks.**

Not surprisingly, perhaps, it is not difficult to find literature in the medical field that directly contradicts the claim that foetuses feel pain and explains why foetal analgesia is used. The following is taken from the British Medical Association's pamphlet *The law and ethics of abortion: BMA views*, published in September 2020:

> A note on fetal pain
>
> Whether, and at what stage a fetus feels pain has been a matter of much debate. The RCOG 2010 report *Fetal Awareness – Review of Research and Recommendations for Practice* concluded that the fetus **cannot experience pain prior to 24 weeks'** gestation, as prior to this point, the necessary connections from the periphery to the

cortex are not present. They also found limited evidence to suggest that fetuses can perceive pain after 24 weeks, **and noted increasing evidence to suggest that the fetus never experiences a state of true wakefulness in utero**.

The BMA recommends that doctors should give due consideration to the appropriate measures for minimising the risk of pain, including assessment of the most recent evidence. The BMA suggests that even if there is no incontrovertible evidence that the fetus feels pain, the use of fetal analgesia when carrying out any procedure (whether an abortion or a therapeutic intervention) on the fetus in utero **may go some way in relieving the anxiety of the woman and health professionals**.

Now, it is not clear whether the Christian Institute is being deliberately disingenuous, but we can conclude that, when it comes to information on medical matters regarding abortion, they are being, at the very least, highly selective in the sources to which they refer!

Notice, however, that nothing we have encountered in this section has any relevance, at all, on the morality of abortion. What I have attempted to do is to show that, when encountering people, or groups, with a specific agenda, they may not be the most objective sources of information.

With that caveat in mind, we can now examine the source of much Christian *authority* – the Bible.

Chapter 2

Abortion and the Bible

God said it. I believe it. THAT SETTLES IT! *Seen on a bumper sticker in the USA.*

Properly read, the Bible is the most potent force for atheism ever conceived. *Isaac Asimov (1920–92) Biochemist and Author*

I stated, in the Introduction, that the Bible makes no direct reference to abortion at all. But before looking at passages that some Christians claim to have relevance for this topic, I need to clarify two issues affecting any understanding of Biblical passages, i.e. Biblical inerrancy and Bible translations.

Many Christian groups, still believe and maintain that the Bible is inerrant and does not contain any contradictions. The Christian Institute is one such group. Their web page, entitled *Who we are*, contains the following:

> We are committed to upholding the truths of the Bible which we believe is inerrant and the supreme authority for all of life.

This continued claim of Biblical inerrancy is somewhat surprising considering that it is so easy to disprove. Pointing out the numerous errors and contradictions contained in the Bible is beyond the scope of this book[18], but a quick comparison of the resurrection accounts in Matthew's and Luke's gospels should be enough to convince all but the most indoctrinated believer that the Bible does, in fact, contain contradictions and, therefore, cannot be inerrant.

First read Matthew 28 in your preferred version of the Bible and answer the following questions:

- Who went to the tomb?
- Was the stone still covering the entrance to the tomb?
- Who did the women see there?
- What did the angel/two men tell them?
- What did the disciples do?
- Where did Jesus appear to them?
- What did Jesus tell the disciples to do?

Now read Luke 24 in the same version of the Bible and compare this account with your answers to the above questions. Anyone attempting to explain away the contradictions as eyewitness confusion is, to say the least, grasping at straws! For example, it would be difficult for eyewitnesses to confuse an angel descending from heaven and rolling back the stone, with two men

---

[18] Anyone interested could pursue this further by reading, for example, *Self-Contradictions of the Bible* by William Henry Burr; *101 Myths of the Bible – How Ancient Scribes Invented Biblical History* by Gary Greenberg, *Misquoting Jesus* by Bart D. Ehrman and *Biblical Nonsense – A Review of the Bible for Doubting Christians* by Dr Jason Long.

inside an already opened tomb, Likewise, in Matthew's account both the angel and then Jesus instruct Mary Magdalene and "the other Mary" to tell the disciples that they are to go to Galilee where they will see Jesus. The disciples dutifully go to Galilee where they meet Jesus who gives them, what is now referred to as, the Great Commission. But in Luke's account Jesus appears to the disciples in Jerusalem and instructs them to stay there "until you have been clothed with the power from on High." These two accounts could hardly be more contradictory. If you now compare the resurrection accounts in Mark's and John's Gospels, you will find even more contradictions.

Nevertheless, despite the Bible's blindingly obvious shortcomings with regard to history, science and ethics, many Christians will quote various passages from it in an attempt to justify their beliefs and actions. It is, therefore, necessary to examine these quotes to see if they have any merit.

Before we look at some of the passages, however, it is important to be aware of the distinction between two terms that come from the Greek – **exegesis** and **eisegesis**. **Exegesis** is the critical explanation or interpretation of text, *viz.* attempting to understand what the original author was trying to say. Clearly, the primary goal of exegesis is to try to discern biblical truths and values by an **unbiased** examination of the text. **Eisegesis**, on the other hand, is defined as the interpretation of a text, using one's own ideas. The telling epigram from the Protestant theologian Samuel Werenfels (1657–1740) clearly illustrates that, all too often, apologetical[19] or polemical considerations can greatly influence the results:

> Men open this book [the Bible], their favourite creed in mind; each seeks his own, and each his own doth find.

In order to know what a particular author is saying it is necessary to understand the actual **context** within which his words are written. A simple example will illustrate the problem. In Christian theology there is a clear distinction between the *Creator* (i.e. God) and the *created* (i.e. everything else). With this viewpoint in mind, let's look at the first two verses of Genesis in a popular English Bible:

> [1] In the beginning God created the heaven and the earth. [2] And the earth was without form, and void; and darkness was upon the face of the deep. And the Spirit of God moved upon the face of the waters. *(Genesis 1:1-2 KJV)*

The *King James Study Bible* (1988) explains it thus:

> Creation marks the absolute beginning of the temporal and material world. The traditional **Jewish** and Christian belief is that Genesis 1:1 declares that God created the original heaven and earth from nothing (Lat. *ex nihilo*) and that verse 2 clarifies that when it

---

[19] Apologetics is the branch of Christian theology dealing with its intellectual defence, especially through the rational justification of its beliefs and doctrines. Apologetics are sometimes distinguished from polemics which set out to defend the beliefs of a particular Christian sect.

came from the Creator's hand, the mass was "without form, and void," unformed and without life. The rest of the chapter then explains the process of Creation in detail.

However, Genesis comes from the Hebrew Bible (Tanakh) and when we look at the same verses here, we get a completely different viewpoint:

> [1] When God began to create heaven and earth – [2] the earth being unformed and void, with darkness over the surface of the deep and a wind from God sweeping over the water... *(Genesis 1:1-2 JSB.)*

The *Jewish Study Bible* (2004) explains it thus:

> 2: This clause describes things just before the process of creation began. To modern people, the opposite of created order is "nothing," that is a vacuum. To the ancients, the opposite of the created order was something much worse than "nothing." It was an active, malevolent force we can best term "chaos." In this verse, chaos is envisioned as a dark, undifferentiated mass of water...
>
> In the midrash, Bar Kappara upholds the troubling notion that **the Torah shows that God created the world out of preexistent material**. But other rabbis worry that acknowledging this would cause people to liken God to a king who had built his palace on a garbage dump, thus arrogantly impugning His majesty (Gen. Rab 1.5). In the ancient Near East, however, **to say that a deity had subdued chaos is to give him the highest praise.**

So, if we ignore the context within which a text is written and impose on it our own previously acquired

beliefs, then we are *guilty* of performing eisegesis on it, and trying to make it say what we either expect it to say or want it to say.

Another important point to be aware of is the fact that, when we are reading the Bible, unless we understand Hebrew (Old Testament) or Greek (New Testament), we are reading a translation, and the translation was made by people with their own specific beliefs and opinions. Let us just explore one term which will have considerable importance for what is to follow, *viz.* **soul.**

Before doing so, however, it is necessary to point out that the Christian Bible was composed and compiled over **at least** 800 years[20], by around forty authors, and contains many different genres, e.g. narrative, poetry, gospels, and epistles. It is not, therefore, surprising that these different authors will sometimes use the same term in different ways. This will become apparent as we explore the term **soul.**

If you look up **soul** in a modern dictionary you will see several definitions, e.g.

1. the spiritual part of a person believed to exist after death.
2. a person's inner character, containing their true thoughts and feelings.
3. a person. For example: Don't tell a soul (do not tell anyone).

---

[20] Those who believe that the Pentateuch was written by Moses, will give a much longer time span.

4.   a person of a particular type. For example: You're a brave soul.

Many professing Christians nowadays *assume* that the term **soul,** in the Bible, means something akin to "the spiritual part of a person believed to exist after death" and some can even refer to documentation from their particular Church for justification. For example, Catechism 366, of the Catholic Church, states:

The Church teaches that every spiritual soul is **created immediately by God** – it is not "produced" by the parents – and also that it is **immortal:** it does not perish when it **separates from the body** at death, **and it will be reunited with the body at the final Resurrection.**

And, the Presbyterian Westminster Confession of Faith has the following:

XXXII. Of the State of Men after Death, and of the Resurrection of the Dead.

1. The bodies of men, after death, return to dust, and see corruption: (Gen. 3:19, Acts 13:36) **but their souls, which neither die nor sleep, having an immortal subsistence, immediately return to God who gave them:** (Luke 23:43, Eccl. 12:7) the souls of the righteous, being then made perfect in holiness, are received into the highest heavens, where they behold the face of God, in light and glory, **waiting for the full redemption of their bodies.** (Heb. 12:23, 2 Cor. 5:1,6,8, Phil. 1:23, Acts 3:21, Eph. 4:10) And the souls of the wicked are cast into hell, **where they remain in torments and utter darkness, reserved to the judgment**

of the great day. (Luke 16:23–24, Acts 1:25, Jude 6–7, 1 Pet. 3:19) Beside these two places, for souls separated from their bodies, the Scripture acknowledgeth none.

2. At the last day, such as are found alive shall not die, but be changed: (1 Thess. 4:17, 1 Cor. 15:51–52) and all the dead shall be raised up, with the self-same bodies, and none other (although with different qualities), **which shall be united again to their souls for ever.** (Job 19:26–27, 1 Cor. 15:42–44.)

3. The bodies of the unjust shall, by the power of Christ, be raised to dishonour: the bodies of the just, by His Spirit, unto honour; and be made conformable to His own glorious body. (Acts 24:15, John 5:28–29, 1 Cor. 15:43, Philip. 3:21.)

It is worthwhile pointing out here that, when a statement denies an opposing viewpoint as in – "it is not 'produced' by the parents" – it does so to refute other competing groups who hold that specific opposing viewpoint. Some Christians in the past, and some to this day, believe that God only created Adam's soul, and that all other souls are *generated* from him. This doctrine is called **Traducianism** and we will consider it later.

For now, let's take a popular English Bible, the King James Version (KJV) and look for the first occurrence of the term **soul**. We find it at Genesis 2:7

> [7] And the LORD God formed man of the dust of the ground, and breathed into his nostrils the breath of life; and man became a living soul. *(Genesis 2:7 KJV.)*

If we *assume* that the author of this verse is referring to an immortal soul, capable of existence independent of the body, we would be making a serious mistake. Genesis was originally written in Hebrew, and the word that the KJV translated as **soul** is נֶפֶשׁ (tr. *nephesh*), and *nephesh* has nothing whatsoever to do with an "immortal soul!" Many Bibles now correctly translate *nephesh* as "living being" or "living creature" as we can see by comparing the same verse in the English Standard Version (ESV):

> [7] then the LORD God formed the man of dust from the ground and breathed into his nostrils the breath of life, and the man became a living creature. *(Gen 2:7 ESV.)*

In fact, Genesis 2:7 is not the first occurrence of *nephesh* and it is interesting to see how the KJV translates them:

> [20] And God said, Let the waters bring forth abundantly the moving creature that hath life [*nephesh*], and fowl that may fly above the earth in the open firmament of heaven. *(Genesis 1:20 KJV.)*

> [21] And God created great whales, and every living [*nephesh*] creature that moveth, which the waters brought forth abundantly, after their kind, and every winged fowl after his kind: and God saw that it was good. *(Genesis 1:21 KJV.)*

> [24] And God said, Let the earth bring forth the living [*nephesh*] creature after his kind, cattle, and creeping thing, and beast of the earth after his kind: and it was so. *(Genesis 1:24 KJV.)*

³⁰ And to every beast of the earth, and to every fowl of the air, and to every thing that creepeth upon the earth, wherein there is life [*nephesh*], I have given every green herb for meat: and it was so. *(Genesis 1:30 KJV.)*

Notice that, in the KJV, there appears to be a distinction between *man* and other *living creatures*, in that *man* has a soul but other *living creatures* do not! This particular distinction, however, does not exist in the original Hebrew.

What is interesting is to compare the way exactly the same Hebrew word is translated in the respective Bibles. We can see, in the diagrams below, the differences between the KJV and the ESV when it comes to the Hebrew word נֶפֶשׁ (tr. *nephesh*):

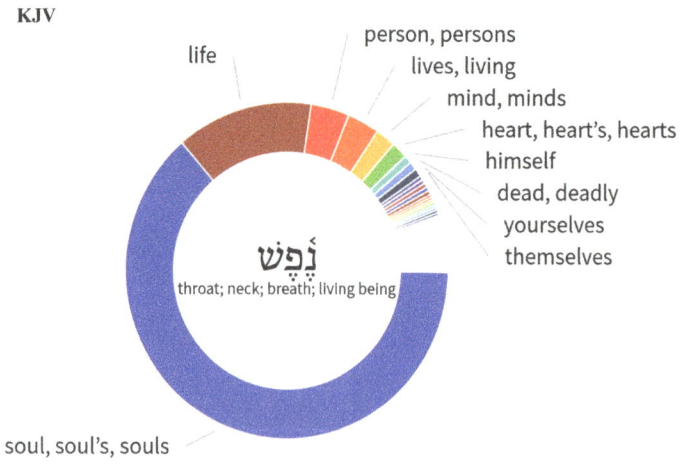

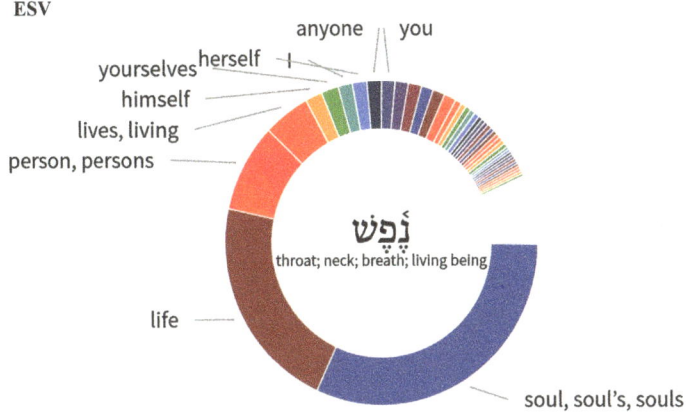

ESV

anyone — you
yourselves herself
himself
lives, living
person, persons

נֶפֶשׁ
throat; neck; breath; living being

life

soul, soul's, souls

This is not to deny that the Hebrew Bible distinguishes between man, who is made in the image of God, and all other living creatures that God gave him dominion over. It is merely to point out that the ancient Hebrews had no concept of an immortal soul that had an existence independent of the death of the body. For them man was not *given* a soul by God; he *became* a soul at birth. In the ancient Hebrew scheme of things, the soul was seen as inseparable from the body. A person was not constituted of a perishable element (the physical body) and a separate immaterial essence (the soul) which was endowed with immortality. Life ceased at that very moment when the breath – which was considered to be loaned by God – was taken back:

> [19] For the fate of humans and the fate of animals is the same; as one dies, so dies the other. They all have the same breath, and humans have no advantage over the animals; for all is vanity. [20] All go to one place; all are from the dust, and all turn to dust again. *(Ecclesiastes 3:19-20 NRS.)*

[29] Thou hidest thy face, they are troubled: thou takest away their breath, they die, and return to their dust. *(Psalms 104:29 KJV.)*

[7] Then shall the dust return to the earth as it was: and the spirit shall return unto God who gave it. *(Ecclesiastes 12:7 KJV.)*

For these early Biblical authors, there could be no victory over death; except that of a state of existence which called for a complete renewal of the human being:

[2] And many of them that sleep in the dust of the earth shall awake, some to everlasting life, and some to shame and everlasting contempt. *(Daniel 12:2 KJV.)*

Notice that the two people who went to heaven, Elijah and Jesus, were taken alive and bodily:

[11] And it came to pass, as they still went on, and talked, that, behold, there appeared a chariot of fire, and horses of fire, and parted them both asunder; and Elijah went up by a whirlwind into heaven. *(2 Kings 2:11 KJV.)*

[50] And he led them out as far as to Bethany, and he lifted up his hands, and blessed them. [51] And it came to pass, while he blessed them, he was parted from them, and carried up into heaven. *(Luke 24:50-51 KJV.)*

Notice also that Luke's Gospel is keen to stress the fact that Jesus' resurrection was not just spiritual but physical – even to the extent that his body consumed food:

³⁶ As they were talking about these things, Jesus himself stood among them, and said to them, "Peace to you!" ³⁷ But they were startled and frightened and thought they saw a spirit. ³⁸ And he said to them, "Why are you troubled, and why do doubts arise in your hearts? ³⁹ See my hands and my feet, that it is I myself. Touch me, and see. For a spirit does not have flesh and bones as you see that I have." ⁴⁰ And when he had said this, he showed them his hands and his feet. ⁴¹ And while they still disbelieved for joy and were marveling, he said to them, "Have you anything here to eat?" ⁴² They gave him a piece of broiled fish, ⁴³ and he took it and ate before them. *(Luke 24:36–43 ESV.)*

We can see this idea, of a person as a psychosomatic unity, in a prayer in the Talmud[21]:

"My God, the soul which Thou **hast placed in me** is pure. Thou hast fashioned it in me, **Thou didst breathe it into me,** and Thou preservest it within me and Thou wilt one day take it from me and restore it to me in the time to come. So long as the soul is within me I give thanks unto Thee, O Lord, my God, and the God of my fathers, Sovereign of all worlds, Lord of all souls. Blessed art Thou, O Lord, **who restorest souls to dead corpses".** *(Berakoth 60b.)*

When we move to the New Testament, which is written mostly in Greek, the Hebrew word *nephesh* is translated into Greek as ψυχή (tr. *psūchê* ≡ "psyche") and, although

---

[21] The Talmud is a collection of ancient rabbinic writings on Jewish law and tradition that constitute the basis of religious authority in Orthodox Judaism.

it can now be separated from the body, it can still be destroyed:

> [28] And fear not them which kill the body, but are not able to kill the soul [psyche]: but rather fear him which is able to destroy both soul [psyche] and body in hell. *(Matthew 10:28 KJV.)*

Understanding the context in which the earliest books of the Bible were written, we can now ask if there is any way we can discern how the authors viewed the **ethical status** of the foetus. Here we can refer to a much-discussed passage in Exodus, from the Jewish Study Bible (JSB):

> [22] When men fight, and one of them pushes a pregnant woman and a miscarriage results, but no other damage ensues, the one responsible shall be fined according as the woman's husband may exact from him, the payment to be based on reckoning. [23] But if other damage ensues, the penalty shall be life for life, [24] eye for eye, tooth for tooth, hand for hand, foot for foot, [25] burn for burn, wound for wound, bruise for bruise. *(Exodus 21:22–25 JSB.)*

Notice that this passage is unambiguous, *viz.* both the "miscarriage" and the "other damage" refer to the woman. The study note also contains the following:

> Halakhic exegesis infers that, since the punishment [for the miscarriage] is monetary rather than execution, the unborn fetus is not considered a living person and feticide is not murder ... hence, abortion is permitted when necessary to save the mother.

I stated that this passage is much discussed because some Christians *believe* that it provides evidence that the Bible does value the life of unborn children and teaches that it is wrong to harm or kill them. For example, the Christian Apologetics & Research Ministry (CARM) has an article on its website, by Luke Wayne, entitled *Does Exodus 21:22-25 justify Abortion?* It contains the following:

> … The phrase ["so that her children come out" or "so that her fruit depart from her"] just means that the child comes out of the womb. If we stick to this plain reading, the passage is distinguishing between a blow that results in the child coming out without injury and a blow that results in the child coming out with an injury. **It would be rather forced to argue that the "with injury" and "without injury" has nothing to do with the child that is being born.** If the child is maimed or killed, the guilty party is physically punished accordingly for having harmed or killed the child. **If not, he still receives a fine for the unintentional assault and the trauma caused to the mother in the premature birth.**
>
> This is the most obvious reading of the Hebrew text, and also makes the most sense in the context. Wounding or killing a grown woman plainly falls under other laws about assault, manslaughter, and murder. The life and health of the unborn child is the only factor unique to the scenario presented here, and so the law focuses its attention there. This is why the majority of modern translators (such as those for the NASB, NKJV, NIV, HSCB, NET, and many others) render the relevant phrase "so that she gives birth prematurely" (or something very similar). It is the most

obvious meaning of the passage. The Mosaic Law, therefore, requires the same punishment for injury done to either the mother or the child. Both lives are held equally precious, and crimes against them are treated just as severe.

Luke Wayne then goes on to talk about the passage in the Septuagint and the Jewish philosopher Philo's interpretation of it.

However, this is a classic case of eisegesis! It should be noted that CARM, as its name clearly states, is a Christian apologetics organization, and it is important to be clear about what apologetics is. *Apologetics* comes from the Greek ἀπολογία (tr. *apologia*), meaning a "verbal defence" or "speech in defence"; so that Christian apologetics is a branch of Christian theology that defends Christianity (or, more usually nowadays, a specific denomination of it) against objections or criticisms. When it comes to the subject of abortion, an apologist sets out to argue for the *belief* that their Church already has. The key element to be aware of here, is that in any debate with them it is not an impartial or objective attempt to seek the truth. As far as an apologist is concerned, they already have the truth, and anyone who holds a different opinion is wrong and needs to be persuaded to change their views; as can be seen by the statement in the article on the CARM website entitled *An Introduction to Apologetics*:

> "Apologetics is the work of convincing people to change their views."

It can be likened to a defence lawyer in a court responding to an argument put forward by the prosecution. Even if the defence is aware of compelling facts in the prosecutions favour, it is certainly not obliged to mention them. My comments about contradictions in the Bible should illustrate the point.

Notice the statement "The Mosaic Law, therefore, requires the same punishment for injury done to either the mother or the child". Well, in fact, in Jewish Law a foetus is not considered a **person**[22] until it begins to egress from the mother during parturition. The rather graphic Ohalot[23] 7:6 makes this unequivocal:

> If a woman has (life-threatening) difficulty in childbirth, one dismembers the embryo within her, limb by limb, **because her life takes precedence over its life.** However, once its head (or its 'greater part') has emerged, it may not be touched, for we do not set aside one **life** for another. *Ohalot 7:6*

This opinion is confirmed in the *Encyclopedia of Jewish Medical Ethics: A Compilation of Jewish Medical Law on All Topics of Medical Interest* (2003). The article on abortion states:

---

[22] Here the term **person** is used to signify a being considered to have the same kind of moral status accorded to children and adults. From here on the context should make clear when we are using the term **person** in this way.

[23] The Ohalot is one of the tractates in the Talmud, considered by Jewish legend as one of the most important.

All Rabbinic opinions agree that the life of the mother takes precedence over that of the fetus. **Their lives have equal status from the moment that the infant emerges.** These facts are deduced from sources in the Mishnah and the Talmud. *(P.5.)*

What most Christians do not know is that, according to Jewish tradition, because Moses' stay on Mount Sinai with God was forty days and forty nights, it was considered too long just to receive the written law. They claim that God also revealed an oral law that Moses passed down, by word of mouth, to Joshua. This oral law eventually got written down in the Mishnah, the Tosephta, and the Babylonian and Jerusalem Talmud's.

The Jewish legal interpretation of this Exodus passage states specifically that only monetary compensation is necessary for one who causes the death of a foetus, which is considered as property of the husband. The unborn foetus is not worthy of the "life for life" punishment demanded if the woman herself is killed. This clearly implies that the foetus is not accorded the same legal status as the woman herself, namely that of an independent human being.

Further proof can be found in the Babylonian Talmud:

MISHNA: In the case of a pregnant woman who is taken by the court to be executed, the court does not wait to execute her until she gives birth. Rather, she is killed immediately. But with regard to a woman taken to be executed who sat on the travailing chair [hamashber] in the throes of labor, the court waits to execute her until she gives birth...

GEMARA: Isn't it obvious that the court executes the pregnant woman rather than waiting? After all, **it is part of her body**. The Gemara answers: It was necessary for the mishna to teach this, as it might enter your mind to say that since it is written: "And if men strive together, and hurt a woman with child, so that her offspring depart...he shall be fined, as the woman's husband shall place upon him" (Exodus 21:22), **the fetus is considered to be the property of the husband.** If so, the court should wait until she gives birth before executing her, **and not cause him to lose the fetus.** Consequently, the mishna teaches us that the court does not take this factor into account...

Rav Yehuda says that Shmuel says: In the case of a pregnant woman who is taken by the court to be executed, one strikes her opposite the womb, i.e., on the abdomen, **so that the fetus dies first and so that she not suffer disgrace as a result of publicly bleeding from labor.** The Gemara asks: Is this to say that according to Shmuel if a pregnant woman dies, she dies first, before the fetus? It is clear that this is Shmuel's assumption, as he mandates killing the fetus before the mother, lest the live fetus bring about the onset of labor as a reaction to the woman's death. Were the fetus to perish first, before the woman, there would be no need for this. But this is difficult, as we maintain that the fetus dies first. *(Arakhim 7a.)*

What is interesting is if we look at a contemporary Jewish view, which can be found in the *Encyclopedia of Judaism (2006)*[24]:

Traditional interpretation of *HALAKHAH*, Jewish Law, allows abortion if the fetus presents a serious

---

[24] In the *Encyclopedia of World Religions* series.

physical threat to the mother, but authorities differ about its permissibility in other cases. *Halakhah* defines full human life as existing only when the head of an infant emerges from the womb...

RASHI, the great 12th-century commentator on the Hebrew Bible (see Torah) and TALMUD, states clearly that the **fetus is not a person**. The Talmud contains the expression "ubar yerech imo – the fetus is **as the thigh of its mother**." In other words, the fetus is deemed to be **part and parcel of the pregnant woman's body**. Therefore, abortion is permitted if the fetus creates a direct threat to the life of the mother.

While there is rabbinic consensus that permits abortion if the fetus presents a physical threat to the mother, there are differing Jewish opinions about whether the psychological health of the mother takes precedence over the pregnancy. Because the Talmud (Yevamot 69b) states that "**the embryo is considered to be mere water until the 40th day**," after which the embryo is considered **partially human** until it is born, many traditional Jews will consider an abortion to be a greater option **prior to the 41st day**.

So, where did this distinction, between an **embryo** up until the 40th day and a **partial human** come from? Well, after the destruction of the temple in Jerusalem in 587/6 BCE, when many Jews were exiled to Babylonia, other Jews began to disperse to many other parts[25]. When Alexander the Great (356 BCE – 323) founded Alexandria in Egypt (332 BCE), it soon became a major centre of Hellenistic culture and a magnet for Jews.

---

[25] This dispersion of the Jews among the Gentiles is referred to as the Jewish Diaspora.

However, the *lingua franca* was Greek and soon there was a need for a Greek version of the Tanakh. The earliest extant translation is the Septuagint (LXX) which was, incidentally, the version from which many early Christians located the prophecies they claimed were fulfilled by Jesus.

However, the Septuagint was not simply a literal translation from the Hebrew. In many places the translators introduced Hellenistic concepts into the text. We can see the effect this had on the passage under discussion:

> [22] And if two men strive and smite a woman with child, and her child be born imperfectly formed, he shall be forced to pay a penalty: as the woman's husband may lay upon him, he shall pay with a valuation. [23] But if it be perfectly formed, he shall give life for life, [24] eye for eye, tooth for tooth, hand for hand, foot for foot, [25] burning for burning, wound for wound, stripe for stripe. *(Exodus 21:22-25 LXX.)*

Notice that the meaning of the text has changed completely, *viz.* the penalty to be exacted depends solely on the status of the foetus; whether it is imperfectly formed or perfectly formed. The matter of any injury to the woman has been entirely removed from consideration. This distinction clearly does not come from the Tanakh but was introduced from Greek philosophy and it subsequently became the cornerstone of an ethically different approach to the status of the foetus. We will take this up in Chapter 4 when we consider the Ontological position.

Having ascertained that early Jews considered the foetus to be nothing more than "part and parcel of the pregnant woman's body" and certainly not a person with independent moral status, we can now look at some of the passages in the Bible that anti-abortionists claim supports their cause, bearing in mind the **context** in which they were written.

In the Christian Institute's *Abortion briefing* 2020, in the section *What the Bible says about abortion*, we get the statement:

> The Psalmist famously praises God because he "created my inmost being… knit me together in my mother's womb". God saw his "unformed body", that is God saw the Psalmist as an embryo.

The references are to Psalm 139:13 and 16. I have reproduced the relevant section from the KJV below:

[13] For thou hast possessed my reins: thou hast covered me in my mother's womb. [14] I will praise thee; for I am fearfully *and* wonderfully made: marvellous *are* thy works; and *that* my soul knoweth right well. [15] My substance was not hid from thee, when I was made in secret, *and* curiously wrought in the lowest parts of the earth. [16] Thine eyes did see my substance, yet being unperfect; and in thy book all *my members* were written, *which* in continuance were fashioned, when *as yet there was* none of them. *(Psalm 139:13-16 KJV.)*

Notice that, what the *briefing* translates as "inmost being," the KJV translates as "reins" (i.e. kidneys). So, what's going on? Well, the Hebrew word is כִּלְיָה

(tr. *kilyah*), which is literally used for the bodily organ of animals and people. For example:

> ¹³ And you shall take all the fat that covers the entrails, and the long lobe of the liver, and the two kidneys [*kilyah*] with the fat that is on them, and burn them on the altar. *(Exodus 29:13 ESV.)*

However, the word can also be used **figuratively** and when used this way is usually translated as "heart" or "inner being." The *Lexham Theological Workbook* (2014) explains it thus:

> The figurative use of כִּלְיָה (*kilyah*) often occurs in poetic parallel with לֵב (*lēb*) as in Jer 11:20; 17:10. These passages reflect a basic level of interchangeability between the two words: Both simply refer to the inner person that can only be fully known to God (compare Psa 7:10). Since English metaphorically uses "heart" to represent one's inner feelings and convictions, the figurative sense of כִּלְיָה (*kilyah*) is often rendered with "heart" or "mind" in English translation. This figurative use for the inner self occurs mainly in poetry and accounts for 9 of the 31 occurrences of the word (Pss 7:9; 16:7; 26:2; 73:21; Prov 23:16; Jer 11:20; 12:2; 17:10; 20:12).

In addition, what the *briefing* translates as "unformed body" and the KJV translates as "substance," is the Hebrew word גֹּלֶם (tr. *Golem*), which literally means "unformed **matter**." According to the Encyclopedia of Judaism, a golem can be described as the Jewish equivalent of the Frankenstein monster. As Dr D A Jones points out, in his book *the soul of the embryo*:

It is striking to note that while this psalm [139] talks eloquently of the moulding of the human **body**, it completely fails to mention the **gift of life or breath**. This is not made explicit because the emphasis of the passage lies not with the gift of life **but with the all-encompassing character of God's knowledge**. The focus is on God's intimate personal understanding of the human individual from the very beginning of his or her existence, to the present and into the future.

Referring back again to the *briefing*, we find:

In Psalm 51:5 David recognises that his need for a Saviour began at the very point of his conception.

Whilst this may be true, if we look at the verse in the Bible, although acknowledging that he was conceived in sin, there is nothing to indicate his moral status as a foetus:

^{5} Behold, I was shapen in iniquity; and in sin did my mother conceive me. *(Psalm 51:5 KJV.)*

As the Bible makes no direct statement about abortion, anyone trying to use it to justify their anti-abortion position must resort to eisegesis and not exegesis. In fact, Christians have been doing this, with the Old Testament, for centuries to justify their claim that Jesus of Nazareth was the Messiah. However, understanding the passages in the context they were written, will soon show how mistaken they were.

For now, I will sum up the early Jewish position as follows:

- After God had created humankind, he instructed them to "Be fruitful and multiply;" a command he repeated to Noah and his sons after the flood (see Genesis 9).

- The initial barrenness of Abraham's wife Sarah, Isaac's wife Rebekah and Jacob's wife Rachel, seems to imply that the ability to conceive children cannot be taken as a given, but is a gift from God.

- Even by the time of Jesus of Nazareth, the world was vastly different than it is today. This was a world without modern medicine, where getting a tooth abscess would probably kill you. In this world every woman of child-bearing age needed to bear an average of five children just to keep the population at a constant level.

- In the Tanakh there are 613 commandments (*mitzvahs*), none of which mentions abortion. Considering the above, it is likely that, if they occurred at all, they were viewed as of so little significance, that it was deemed unnecessary to comment on them.

- Rather than considering a person as being constituted of a perishable element (the physical body) and a separate immaterial essence (the soul) which was endowed with immortality, a person was viewed as a psychosomatic unity only when it began to emerge from its mother.

It is worth noting here that the State of Israel today has one of the most relaxed attitudes to abortion you will find anywhere in the world. In an article published on

22 May 2019, in the online edition of the Haaretz Newspaper[26], we find this:

> Israeli abortion law has something for everyone: A **semblance of regulation** for conservatives, but **a reality in which almost any woman who wants an abortion is able to have one** — and an estimated 40,000 Israeli women annually have them.
>
> For an Israeli woman who wishes to end a pregnancy, **the process is not only legal but is usually heavily subsidized or free,** covered under Israel's national health care system.

Clearly, the Israeli state does not consider abortion as murder!

---

[26] https://www.haaretz.com/israel-news/.premium.MAGAZINE-shhh-don-t-tell-evangelical-supporters-of-israel-about-the-country-s-abortion-laws-1.7274968

Chapter 3

The Perversity Position

Many of the critics of the ban on artificial contraception point out that it is a relic of a context in which women were understood as having been created **solely for the purpose of reproduction,** for as Augustine stated and Thomas Aquinas seconded, **the term helpmate in Genesis could not have meant anything but reproduction "for in any other task a man would be better helped by another man."** *Christine E. Gudorf.*[27]

In the *Introduction* I stated that, historically, there have only ever been two reasons put forward to justify the claim that abortion is morally wrong, i.e. the **perversity position** and the **ontological position.** I will deal with the perversity position first since, as we will see, even some parts of the Roman Catholic Church have altered their stance on it. In addition, many people wrongly believe that the Christian Church has opposed abortion, from its inception, on the conviction that a new human person exists from the moment of conception and that this newly formed person has the same *right to life* as any other person (*viz.* the ontological position). That this is not the case will be shown in detail when we examine the ontological position in the next chapter.

---

[27] From *Sacred Rights: The Case for Contraception and Abortion in World Religions – Contraception and Abortion in Roman Catholicism.*

For now, as we will be examining St Augustine's views, I include the following quote to illustrate his position on early term abortions:

> The law does not provide that the act [abortion] pertains to homicide, **for there cannot yet be said to be a live soul in a body that lacks sensation** when it is not formed in flesh and so is not endowed with sense. *On Exodus.*

Also, consider the following quote from James McCartney's article, *Some Roman Catholic Concepts of Person and Their Implications for the Ontological Status of the Unborn*[28]:

> Many people believe that the Roman Catholic Church's opposition to abortion stems from its conviction that a new human person exists from the first moment of conception and that this newly formed person has as much right to exist as anyone else. It is clear that this **is not now, nor ever has been,** official Church teaching on this matter. Susan Teft Nicholson points out that, besides its ethic proscribing killing, "Roman Church leadership has sought to maintain, in one form or another, a link between sexual activity and procreation, **and thus it follows that even if the fetus were not a human being, Catholics would still view abortion as evil**".

Before examining the perversity position itself, however, I want to put it into the form of a simple logical

---

[28] In *Abortion and the Status of the Fetus: Philosophy and Medicine volume 13* (1983)

argument. It will then be a straightforward matter to determine whether it is **valid** and/or **sound**. A **valid** argument is one where, if the premises are true then the conclusion must also be true. A **sound** argument is a valid argument where the premises are true. Clearly, a sound argument is the strongest and most convincing of all possible arguments as, if you have truly constructed a sound argument, then the conclusion is *necessarily* and *universally* true, whether other people choose to accept it or not.

The perversity position can logically be argued thus:

P1. Sexual intercourse is solely for the purpose of procreation.

P2. Anything that interferes with, or prevents, the sexual act from producing children is morally wrong.

P3. Abortion prevents the sexual act from producing children.

Therefore

C. Abortion is morally wrong.

As abortion certainly prevents the sexual act from producing children, **P3** is true and inviolable. But if **P1** and **P2** are true, then not only is abortion immoral, as are homosexual sex and sex within marriage when one of the partners is sterile, but also **all** forms of contraception including married couples having sex at a time of the month when conception is thought unlikely (the rhythm method) are immoral as well. As this latter prohibition has a far greater impact on family life, I want to examine it here.

As with the concept of the *immortal soul*, the idea that sexual intercourse is solely for the purpose of procreation did not come into Christianity from scripture – nowhere in the Old Testament will you find a condemnation of contraception – but from pagan philosophy, specifically Stoicism.

For example, the Stoic philosopher Gaius Musonius Rufus (*c.* 30–*c.* 101 CE), considered by many the *Roman Socrates*, wrote:

> Men who are not wantons or immoral are bound to consider sexual intercourse justified only when it occurs in marriage and is indulged in **for the purpose of begetting children**, since that is lawful, but unjust and unlawful when it is mere pleasure-seeking, even in marriage. *On sexual indulgence.*

It was St Augustine (354–430), described by the *Encyclopaedia Britannica* as "perhaps the most significant Christian thinker after St Paul," who was the most authoritative writer on the perversity position. To say that he had a negative view of sex – identifying it almost unequivocally with lust – is somewhat of an understatement. For Augustine sex, even within marriage, was a necessary evil, required only for procreation, as these passages from *On Marriage and Concupiscence* show:

> Nevertheless, conjugal intercourse is not in itself sin, **when it is had with the intention of producing children**; because the mind's good-will leads the ensuing bodily pleasure, instead of following its lead; and the human choice is not distracted by the yoke of sin pressing

upon it, inasmuch as the blow of the sin is rightly brought back to the purposes of procreation. *Book 1, Chapter 13.*

It is, however, one thing for married persons to have intercourse **only for the wish to beget children,** which is not sinful; **it is another thing for them to desire carnal pleasure in cohabitation,** but with the spouse only, which involves venial [pardonable] sin. For although propagation of offspring is not the motive of the intercourse, **there is still no attempt to prevent such propagation,** wither by wrong desire or **evil appliance.** They who resort to these, although called by the name of spouses, are really not such; **they retain no vestige of true matrimony** but pretend the honourable designation as a cloak for criminal conduct. *Book 1, Chapter 17.*

Augustine is the first leading Christian to speak in general terms of birth control measures within marriage, claiming that even married couples who engage in intercourse and attempt to prevent offspring are like fornicators and adulterers. And, until 1930 there had been a general Christian prohibition on contraception.

What is noteworthy, however, is to see how religious attitudes can change over relatively short periods of time, even within one religious' group. For example, Anglicans regularly hold a *Lambeth Conference* during which *Resolutions* are made and voted on. As the following extracts show, in 1908 they condemned the practice of contraception as "demoralising to character and hostile to national welfare", but gradually over fifty years, and with concerns over global overpopulation, they determine that it's the responsibility of the parents to decide upon "the number and frequency of children":

The Conference regards with alarm the growing practice of the artificial restriction of the family, and earnestly calls upon all Christian people to discountenance the use of all artificial means of restriction as **demoralising to character** and **hostile to national welfare.** *Resolution 41, 1908.*

We utter an emphatic warning against the use of unnatural means for the avoidance of conception, together with the grave dangers - physical, moral and religious - thereby incurred, and against the evils with which the extension of such use threatens the race. In opposition to the teaching which, under the name of science and religion, encourages married people in the deliberate cultivation of sexual union as an end in itself, **we steadfastly uphold what must always be regarded as the governing considerations of Christian marriage. One is the primary purpose for which marriage exists, namely the continuation of the race through the gift and heritage of children;** the other is the paramount importance in married life of deliberate and thoughtful self-control. *Resolution 68, 1920.*

However, move forward ten years and we find the Anglican church becoming the first mainline Christian denomination to officially endorse contraception, albeit in limited circumstances only:

Where there is clearly felt moral obligation to limit or avoid parenthood, the method must be decided on Christian principles. The primary and obvious method is complete abstinence from intercourse (as far as may be necessary) in a life of discipline and self-control lived in the power of the Holy Spirit. **Nevertheless in those cases where there is such a clearly felt moral obligation to limit or avoid parenthood, and where**

> **there is a morally sound reason for avoiding complete abstinence, the Conference agrees that other methods may be used, provided that this is done in the light of the same Christian principles.** The Conference records its strong condemnation of the use of any methods of conception control from motives of selfishness, luxury, or mere convenience. *Resolution 15, 1930.*

And, by 1958 church leaders have now concluded that God has endowed parents with the intelligence to decide for themselves the number of children to have and the spacing between them:

> The Conference believes that the responsibility for deciding upon the number and frequency of children has been laid by God upon the consciences of parents everywhere; that this planning, in such ways as are mutually acceptable to husband and wife in Christian conscience, is a right and important factor in Christian family life and should be the result of positive choice before God. Such responsible parenthood, built on obedience to all the duties of marriage, requires a wise stewardship of the resources and abilities of the family as well as a thoughtful consideration of the varying population needs and problems of society and the claims of future generations. *Resolution 115, 1958.*

Interestingly, the 1930 conference prompted the Roman Catholic Pope Pius XI (1857–1939) to circulate an encyclical[29], *Casti connubii* (Lat. "of chaste wedlock"), reaffirming his church's position against, amongst other

---

[29] A letter from the Pope sent to all Roman Catholic bishops throughout the world.

things, artificial birth control and abortion. His condemnation of those who use contraception seems very Augustinian:

> 54. But no reason, however grave, may be put forward by which anything **intrinsically against nature** may become conformable to nature and morally good. Since, therefore, **the conjugal act is destined primarily by nature for the begetting of children**, those who in exercising it deliberately frustrate its natural power and purpose **sin against nature** and commit **a deed which is shameful and intrinsically vicious.**

> 56. Since, therefore, openly departing from the **uninterrupted Christian tradition** some [i.e. Anglicans] recently have judged it possible solemnly to declare another doctrine regarding this question, the Catholic Church, to whom God has entrusted the defense of the integrity and purity of morals, **standing erect in the midst of the moral ruin which surrounds her,** in order that she may preserve the chastity of the nuptial union **from being defiled by this foul stain,** raises her voice in token of her divine ambassadorship and through Our mouth proclaims anew: **any use whatsoever of matrimony exercised in such a way that the act is deliberately frustrated in its natural power to generate life is an offense against the law of God and of nature, and those who indulge in such are branded with the guilt of a grave sin.**

So, we now have two major Christian denominations disagreeing over the permissibility of contraception! However, consider the following passage in the same encyclical:

59.... Nor are those considered as acting against nature who in the married state use their right in the proper manner although **on account of natural reasons either of time or of certain defects,** new life cannot be brought forth. For in matrimony as well as in the use of the matrimonial rights there are also secondary ends, such as mutual aid, the cultivating of mutual love, and the quieting of concupiscence which husband and wife are not forbidden to consider so long as they are subordinated to the primary end and so long as the intrinsic nature of the act is preserved.

The phrase "natural reasons either of time or of certain defects" was universally accepted as signifying menopause and infertility, meaning that menopausal women and infertile couples could morally engage in intercourse even though there was no possibility of children resulting from the act. However, some Catholics took *natural reasons of time* to also mean the infertile portion of a woman's menstrual cycle, opening the door for Catholics to morally use the rhythm method, a practice given legitimacy, in 1951, by Pope Pius XII (1876–1958), providing adequate grounds for a couple to limit the size of their family. Subsequently, this was to cause serious consequences for the papacy, around the time of Vatican II[30], as it accepted a separation between the sexual act itself and its procreative *purpose.*

When Pope John XXIII (1881–1963) convoked Vatican II[31], to commence in 1962, he did not want the almost

---

[30] The twenty-first ecumenical council 1962–65.
[31] On 25 December 1961.

three thousand bishops and other clerics, due to attend, to address the birth control issue even though there were pressing pastoral reasons for doing so.

The general dissatisfaction and unreliability of the rhythm method, concern over the worldwide population boom and the introduction of the birth control pill to the public in early 1960, along with various other factors, led many Catholics to argue for a reconsideration of their church's position on family planning and contraception. Could there, for example, be a case for taking the procreative responsibility of a married couple over the totality of their married life, instead of each individual act of sexual intimacy? Also, because it used **naturally** occurring hormones to mimic the infertile periods in the menstrual cycle, could the birth control pill be a morally acceptable alternative to the rhythm method?

So, in order to find answers to these and other questions, Pope John XXIII appointed *The Papal Birth Control Commission*[32], in April 1963, comprising six non-theologians (two doctors, a sociologist, a demographer, a diplomat, and an economist). After his death later that year, the commission continued under the aegis of Pope Paul VI (1897–1978) who, over the next three years, expanded it to seventy-two members, including sixteen theologians.

In June 1966 the commission produced a report, entitled *Responsible Parenthood*, intended to convince the Pope

---

[32] Formally known as the Pontifical Commission for the Study of Population, Family and Births.

that a change in Church teaching could be reconciled with tradition and that the procreative responsibility of a married couple could be considered over the totality of their married life:

> The large amount of knowledge and facts which throw light **on today's world** suggest that it is **not to contradict the genuine sense of this tradition** and the purpose of the previous doctrinal condemnations if we speak of the regulation of conception by using means, human and decent, ordered **to favoring fecundity in the totality of married life** and toward the realization of the authentic values of a fruitful matrimonial community.
>
> The reasons in favor of this affirmation are of several kinds: social changes in matrimony and the family, especially in the role of the woman; lowering of the infant mortality rate; new bodies of knowledge in biology, psychology, sexuality and demography; a changed estimation of the value and meaning of human sexuality and of conjugal relations; most of all, a better grasp of the duty of man to humanize and to bring to greater perfection for the life of man what is given in nature. **Then must be considered the sense of the faithful: according to it, condemnation of a couple to a long and often heroic abstinence as the means to regulate conception, cannot be founded on the truth.**

The report goes on to mention the acceptance of the rhythm method, which creates a separation between a sexual act itself and its possible reproductive consequence:

> The notion of responsible parenthood which is implied in the notion of a prudent and generous regulation of

conception, advanced in Vatican Council II, had already been prepared by Pius XII. **The acceptance of a lawful application of the calculated sterile periods of the woman**—that the application is legitimate presupposes right motives—**makes a separation between the sexual act which is explicitly intended and its reproductive effect which is intentionally excluded.**

The report authors were also keen to point out a distinction between a *contraceptive mentality* "egotistically and irrationally opposed to fruitfulness", which the Catholic Church had traditionally rejected, and a married couple using the products of man's ingenuity and skill to responsibly plan their family:

> The tradition has always rejected seeking this separation with a contraceptive intention for motives spoiled by egoism and hedonism, and such seeking can never be admitted. The true opposition is not to be sought between some material conformity to the physiological processes of nature and some artificial intervention. **For it is natural to man to use his skill in order to put under human control what is given by physical nature.** The opposition is really to be sought between one way of acting which is contraceptive and opposed to a prudent and generous fruitfulness, and another way which is, in an ordered relationship to responsible fruitfulness and which has a concern for education and all the essential, human and Christian values.

Making the point that artificial birth control was not *intrinsically evil*, and that married couples should be allowed to decide for themselves the timing and number of children, the report was intended to be the definitive word of the Commission to be given to Pope Paul VI.

However, the American Jesuit theologian John Ford (1902 – 1989) decided to produce a report representing the opposing view, which he sent to the pope behind the back of the rest of the commission. This report – *The State of the Question: The Doctrine of the Church and Its Authority* – signed by only four members of the commission, was not based on any ethical foundation but on the foreseeable consequences for the Roman Catholic church:

"If it should be declared," they wrote, "that contraception is not evil in itself, then we should have to concede frankly that the Holy Spirit had been on the side of the Protestant churches in 1930 (when the encyclical *Casti connubii* was promulgated), in 1951 (Pius XII's address to the midwives), and in 1958 (the address delivered before the Society of Hematologists in the year the pope died). It should likewise have to be admitted that for a half a century the Spirit failed to protect Pius XI, Pius XII, and a large part of the Catholic hierarchy from a very serious error. This would mean that the leaders of the church, acting with extreme imprudence, had condemned thousands of innocent human acts, forbidding, under pain of eternal damnation, a practice which would now be sanctioned. The fact can neither be denied nor ignored that these same acts would now be declared licit on the grounds of principles cited by the Protestants, which popes and bishops have either condemned, or at least not approved." *How the Pope Became Infallible: Pius IX and the Politics of Persuasion, p.270*[33].

---

[33] This book was originally published in German under the title *Wie Der Papst Unfehlbar Wurde: Macht und Ommacht eines Dogmas* in 1979. Translated by Peter Heinegg 1981.

Given this report, it is perhaps unsurprising that Pope Paul VI rejected the commission's recommendations in his first encyclical, *Humanae Vitae*[34], dated 25 July 1968, stating:

> 6. However, the conclusions arrived at by the commission could not be considered by Us as definitive and absolutely certain, dispensing Us from the duty of examining personally this serious question. This was all the more necessary because, within the commission itself, there was not complete agreement concerning the moral norms to be proposed, and especially because certain approaches and criteria for a solution to this question had emerged which were at variance with the moral doctrine on marriage constantly taught by the magisterium of the Church.

The encyclical then goes on to confirm that, whilst infertile couples can morally engage in sexual activity "every marital act must of necessity retain its intrinsic relationship to the procreation of human life" although, rather contradictorily, the rhythm method may be employed:

> 11. The sexual activity, in which husband and wife are intimately and chastely united with one another, through which human life is transmitted, is, as the recent Council recalled, "noble and worthy." (11) It does not, moreover, **cease to be legitimate even when, for reasons independent of their will, it is foreseen to be infertile.** For its natural adaptation to the expression and strengthening of the union of husband and wife is

---

[34] Lat. *On Human Life.*

not thereby suppressed. The fact is, as experience shows, that new life is not the result of each and every act of sexual intercourse. God has wisely ordered laws of nature and the incidence of fertility in such a way that successive births are already naturally spaced through the inherent operation of these laws. The Church, nevertheless, **in urging men to the observance of the precepts of the natural law,** which it interprets by its constant doctrine, teaches that **each and every marital act must of necessity retain its intrinsic relationship to the procreation of human life.** (12)

16. ... If therefore there are well-grounded reasons for spacing births, arising from the physical or psychological condition of husband or wife, or from external circumstances, **the Church teaches that married people may then take advantage of the natural cycles immanent in the reproductive system and engage in marital intercourse only during those times that are infertile,** thus controlling birth in a way which does not in the least offend the moral principles which We have just explained. (20)

I'll leave you to draw your own conclusions as to why the papacy is still holding to the position stated in *Casti connubii*, but a 2008 study by the Tablet magazine[35], which surveyed 1,500 Mass-goers in England and Wales, found that the contraceptive pill is used by 54.5% and nearly 69% had used or would consider using condoms. The survey also found that more than half think that the teaching on contraception should be revised.

---

[35] A weekly Catholic news magazine.

Without surveying all of the, over 30,000, other Christian denominations in the world, we can see that some teach that it is acceptable to use birth control as long as it is not used to permit or encourage promiscuous behaviour. For example, the Methodist Church has this statement under the question What about contraception? [36]:

> The Methodist Church believes that responsible contraception is **a welcome means** towards fulfilment in marriage, the spacing of children, and the need to avoid pregnancy altogether, for example for medical reasons.

And the United Methodist Church's Resolution on Responsible Parenthood[37] , has this:

> Each couple **has the right** and the duty prayerfully and responsibly to control conception according to their circumstances. They are, in our view, **free to use those means of birth control considered medically safe**. As developing technologies have moved conception and reproduction more and more out of the category of a chance happening and more closely to the realm of responsible choice, **the decision whether or not to give birth to children must include acceptance of the responsibility to provide for their mental, physical, and**

---

[36] https://www.methodist.org.uk/about-us/the-methodist-church/views-of-the-church/abortion-and-contraception/

[37] https://web.archive.org/web/20070509041351/http://www.umc-gbcs.org/site/apps/nl/content3.asp?c=fsJNK0PKJrH&b=848309&content_id=%7BD78C069C-1151-4E3C-8840-B707FC4B96EF%7D&notoc=1

spiritual growth, as well as consideration of the possible effect on quality of life for family and society.

To support the sacred dimensions of personhood, all possible efforts should be made by parents and the community to ensure that each child enters the world with a healthy body and is born into an environment conducive to the realization of his or her full potential.

As we only find the perversity position in Christianity, I have not commented on other religions in detail, but Jews, Muslims, Buddhists, Hindus and Sikhs all accept, at least, some forms of contraception[38].

In this chapter, we have seen that Christian ideas about contraception did not come from Scripture, but from various church teachings imported from stoic philosophy. And, although all major denominations disapproved of artificial contraception until the Lambeth Conference in 1930, different groups now hold various views about the morality of using birth control.

We can, therefore, conclude that neither **P1** nor **P2** are objective factual statements, with correspondingly *true* values. They are simply opinions held by some conservative Christians. This being the case, the argument for the perversity position is **unsound** and can be rejected.

---

[38] https://www.fpa.org.uk/factsheets/religion-contraception-and-abortion-factsheet

Chapter 4

The Ontological View

There is simply no way the state can be neutral on the question of when **life begins**, because if there can be any laws at all that protect **human beings**, the state has to make a decision on who counts as a **human being** and who doesn't under those laws. Pro-life advocates simply maintain that the state should endorse an answer to the question of when **life begins**, or who counts as a **human being** with a **right to life**, that is backed **by science** and **common sense**. *Trent Horn, Catholic apologist*

Once the argument for the perversity view against abortion has been shown to be unsound, anti-abortionists are only left with arguments for the ontological view. Before examining this view in detail, a few comments will, I hope, lay the foundations for our investigation.

In his book *Persuasive Pro-Life*, from which the under-heading quote is taken, Trent Horn advises other people on different *techniques* and *arguments* they can employ when debating various *types* of people abortion. The quote comes in Chapter 4, where he is advising on how to deal with the *Tolerant type*, *viz.* whilst this personality type does not like abortion, they *tolerate* it because they believe other people should be able to choose it.

The following quote is from Chapter 6, where he is giving advice on how to deal with the *type* he refers to as *Skeptics*:

> **Your objective:** Show that there is no doubt the unborn child is a **biological human being** and that the debate over the status of the unborn child involves **philosophy, not science.**

Now, Trent Horn is a Catholic apologist and, as we saw in Chapter 2, an apologist's goal is to get those with a different viewpoint to change their minds. You should not, therefore, expect an unbiased presentation of the facts, to say the least. For example, notice that his attitude to science appears to change depending on who he is trying to convince!

The reason I mention this is because an apologist will often use arguments that are completely irrelevant to the matter at hand. For example, nowadays, I doubt if you will find anyone defending the right of a woman to have an abortion stating that a zygote, blastocyst, embryo or foetus is not either:

- alive from the moment of fertilization.
- a *biological* human being from the moment of fertilization.

These are matters of **fact** that science can, and has, answered; zygotes, blastocysts, embryos, and foetuses are all *biologically* human – they are recognizable developmental stages of the species *Homo sapiens*. The disagreement is over their **moral status** and any **rights** they may have as a result of their moral status. Does, for example, an embryo have the same *right to life* as the woman whose body it is *inhabiting*? Is the woman's *right to bodily autonomy* sufficient to permit her to have an abortion?

Unfortunately, such questions are not, as Trent Horn suggests, simply matters of **common sense**. If they were, then most people would probably have stopped arguing about them long ago. He is quite correct, however, when he states that "the status of the unborn child involves philosophy, not science". The fact is that, although science can be extremely useful in informing the decisions of policymakers on several matters, we cannot use it to decide whether abortion is **morally** right or wrong.

In some respect, the term *ontological view* is a bit of a misnomer, because it only covers part of the argument. For those not familiar with the various branches of philosophy, it is important to know that **Ontology** is a branch of **Metaphysics** that, simply put, studies the nature of **being** and **existence**. So, it is legitimate to ask: Ontologically, what is a human being? And we will be looking at how Christian's have answered this question below. But now consider the following logical argument:

P1. Humans feel pain if you hit them.
P2. John is a human.
Therefore
C. You ought not to hit John.

Anyone new to logic may be surprised to learn that this simple argument is **not valid**! The reason being is that the conclusion does not logically follow from the two premises. You cannot derive normative statements, *viz.* statements which describe how the world *ought* to be, directly from descriptive statements, which describe how the world actually *is*. This was first highlighted by the Scottish philosopher David Hume (1711–76) and, although the difficulty is usually referred to as the **is-ought problem**, it is also known as Hume's Law or Hume's Guillotine. No matter how many descriptive statements we add to the above argument, the normative conclusion will still not follow. For example,

P1. Humans feel pain if you hit them.
P2. John is a human.
P3. Pain is a form of suffering.
P4. John does not want to suffer.
Therefore
C. You ought not to hit John.

This argument is still not valid. The only way to derive the normative conclusion, in the examples, would be to add at least one normative statement such as **Px.** You ought not to inflict pain on humans, into the list of premises.

When we start talking about *ought/ought not*, *right/ wrong* and *good/bad*, we have entered another realm of philosophy called **Ethics**, and it is important that we do not inadvertently cross the *chasm* between ontology and ethics without realising it. That this is all too easily done, can be seen with the following example:

P1. A foetus is a *human being*.

P2. Killing innocent *human beings* is morally wrong.

P3. Abortion is the killing of a foetus.

Therefore

C. Abortion is morally wrong.

This argument is undeniably **valid**, which means that if its three premises are all true then the conclusion *necessarily* follows and must also be true. However, this argument contains a **fallacy** which, unless you are already aware of it, is not easy to spot. It is called a **fallacy of equivocation** and arises when a term is used with two different meanings. In this argument, the first premise is using the term *human being* to claim that a foetus is a member of the species *homo sapiens* which, of course, it is. This is a *factual* claim that cannot be refuted; a foetus is biologically human.

However, the second premise is making a *moral* claim about innocent *human beings*. Now, whilst, usually, innocent human beings are ethically classed as *moral agents*, with a *right to life*, we cannot *assume* that a foetus automatically has this same moral status, as this is what the anti-abortionist is trying to claim in the first place!

One way of avoiding such errors is to use one term when referring to **facts**, and another when discussing **values** and **rights**. Because, in biology, the term **human being** has a precise meaning, i.e. it refers to an entity of the species *Homo sapiens*, from now on I will use this term in its strictly biological sense. This will allow me to talk about a **human being** existing from the moment of fertilization, without the term carrying any religious, ethical, or legal connotations. Similarly, as **person** is defined as a legal entity recognized by law as having rights and duties, I will use this term when referring to an entities' moral and/or legal status, *viz.* a **person** is an entity who is entitled to specific legal protections, and **personhood** denotes the state of enjoying those protections.

With this distinction in mind, we can look at the ontological question: What is a human being? First, we can see what Christians claim a human being is, and then examine that claim to see how it aligns with what modern embryology can tell us.

We saw, in Chapter 2, that the earliest Biblical notion of a person was that of a psychosomatic unity **only once it had begun to emerge from its mother**. However, the majority Christian view is that a person is a combination of a material human body and a spiritual immortal soul[39]. For example:

> The **human person,** created in the image of God, is a being **at once corporeal and spiritual**... *Catechism 362.*

> The human body shares in the dignity of "the image of God": it is a human body **precisely because it is animated by a spiritual soul,** and it is the whole **human**

---

[39] Although this is the general view among Christians, it is by no means universal. Some Christians are *monists*, maintaining that human beings, consist solely of one physical substance.

person that is intended to become, in the body of Christ, a temple of the Spirit: *Catechism 364*.

As this idea clearly did not come from early Hebrew scripture, we need to explore where it came from and how it developed within Christian theology.

Although the origins of a soul separate from the body predates Western philosophy, the idea actually filtered into Christianity through Greek (i.e. pagan!) philosophy. A little history will clarify the situation.

As early as the Greek poet Homer, thought to have flourished 9th to 8th century BCE, the word *soul* was used to refer to something that a human being risks in battle and loses at death, when it travels to the underworld, where it exists as an image (or shade[40]) of the deceased person. For Homer, the presence of a soul endows a person with life, but is not responsible for the behaviour, motivations, feelings or moral character of that life. Also, only human beings had (and, thus, could lose) souls.

Significant changes in thinking about the soul began to emerge in Ancient Greece around the sixth and fifth centuries BCE. At about this time the adjective *empsuchos* (ensouled) began to be employed to mean 'alive'. However, it was not used just in relation to human beings but in relation to all things considered to

---

[40] We can see a parallel of this in the Hebrew idea of *shades* (rephaim) in the underworld (Sheol). See, for example, Isaiah 14:9 and Job 26:5-6.

be alive. Hence, the philosopher Thales of Miletus (*fl.* sixth century BCE) thought that, since it is distinctive of living things to be able to initiate movement, lodestone and amber must be ensouled. Gradually, the concept of soul began to develop further and, by the end of the fifth century, soul was not only thought of as the distinguishing attribute of living things but, in man, as something responsible for thinking, planning and moral character.

For the philosopher Plato (428/427–348/347 BCE), the soul and the body were two distinct entities, with the soul being immortal and existing in the "heavens" before birth, but after a "fall" to Earth being "imprisoned" in a body. Consider these extracts from his Phaedo[41] and how they compare to the Christian statements in Chapter 2:

> Do we believe that there is such a thing as death?...
>
> And is this anything but **the separation of soul and body**? And being dead is the attainment of this separation; **when the soul exists in herself**, and is parted from the body and the body is parted from the soul...
>
> Then reflect, Cebes: is not the conclusion of the whole matter this? – that the soul is in the very likeness of the divine, and immortal, and intelligible, and uniform, and indissoluble, and unchangeable; and the body is in the very likeness of the human, and mortal, and unintelligible, and multiform, and dissoluble, and changeable...

---

[41] From: http://classics.mit.edu/Plato/phaedo.html

Now, remember that Jesus and his earliest disciples were Jews. Thus, early Christianity was based on the notion of resurrection of the dead, *viz.* resurrection of the body. For these first Christians, no part of them was immortal, and when they died, they were one hundred percent dead. However, the hope that is taught in the New Testament is a hope for resurrection; or as the Apostle Paul refers to it as being raised to newness of life in Christ. We can see this, most graphically, in Matthew's Gospel after Jesus has died:

> [50] Then Jesus cried again with a loud voice and breathed his last. [51] At that moment the curtain of the temple was torn in two, from top to bottom. The earth shook, and the rocks were split. [52] The tombs also were opened, and many bodies of the saints who had fallen asleep were raised. [53] After his resurrection they came out of the tombs and entered the holy city and appeared to many. *(Matthew 27:50–53 NRS.)*

The Greek word καθεύδω (tr. koimaō) is translated in the NRS (and most other English Bibles) as "fallen asleep" and was a common euphemism for "died."

We appear, therefore, to have two seemingly incompatible doctrines, *viz.* immortality of the soul and resurrection. So, how did Plato's idea of an immortal soul get incorporated into Christian theology?

Considered by the *Encyclopaedia Britannica* as the most important theologian and biblical scholar of the early Greek church, Origen (*c.*185–*c.*254) was the first person to attempt to organize Christian doctrine into a systematic theology. He was an admirer of Plato and believed in the immortality of the soul. In his *De Principiis* (On the First Principles), he wrote:

> ... the soul, **having a substance and life of its own**, shall, after its departure from the world, be rewarded according to its deserts, being destined to obtain either an inheritance of eternal life and blessedness, if its actions shall have procured this for it, or to be delivered up to eternal fire and punishments, if the guilt of its crimes shall have brought it down to this: and also, that there is to be a time of resurrection from the dead, when this body, which now "is sown in corruption, shall rise in incorruption," and that which "is sown in dishonour will rise in glory."

Although not universal among Christians today, it is generally believed that, at death they go immediately to Heaven to be with God – the Platonist part of the doctrine – where they wait for the Day of Judgment, when their souls will be reunited with their bodies – the resurrection part of the doctrine.

We can see this, for example, in the section of the Presbyterian Westminster Confession of Faith, quoted in Chapter 2:

> XXXII. Of the State of Men after Death, and of the Resurrection of the Dead
>
> 1. The bodies of men, after death, return to dust, and see corruption: (Gen. 3:19, Acts 13:36) but their souls, **which neither die nor sleep**, having **an immortal subsistence**, immediately return to God who gave them: (Luke 23:43, Eccl. 12:7) **the souls of the**

righteous, being then made perfect in holiness, are received into the highest heavens, where they behold the face of God, in light and glory, waiting for the full redemption of their bodies. (Heb. 12:23, 2 Cor. 5:1,6,8, Phil. 1:23, Acts 3:21, Eph. 4:10) **And the souls of the wicked are cast into hell,** where they remain in torments and utter darkness, **reserved to the judgment of the great day**. (Luke 16:23–24, Acts 1:25, Jude 6–7, 1 Pet. 3:19) Beside these two places, for souls separated from their bodies, the Scripture acknowledgeth none.

2. At the last day, such as are found alive shall not die, but be changed: (1 Thess. 4:17, 1 Cor. 15:51–52) **and all the dead shall be raised up, with the self-same bodies,** and none other (although with different qualities), **which shall be united again to their souls for ever.** (Job 19:26–27, 1 Cor. 15:42–44.)

3. The bodies of the unjust shall, by the power of Christ, be raised to dishonour: the bodies of the just, by His Spirit, unto honour; and be made conformable to His own glorious body. (Acts 24:15, John 5:28–29, 1 Cor. 15:43, Philip. 3:21.)

And Catechism 997 of the Catholic Church describes it thus:

What is "rising"? In death, **the separation of the soul from the body**, the human body decays and **the soul goes to meet God**, while awaiting its reunion with its glorified body. God, in his almighty power, will definitively grant incorruptible life to our bodies **by reuniting them with our soul**, through the power of Jesus Resurrection.

Now, although each immortal soul was/is believed to come from God, there was, and continues to be, considerable disagreement as to when it was/is created and when it was/is *infused* into a body. The three relevant doctrines are called **Creationism, Pre-existence**, and **Traducianism** (which was introduced in Chapter 2).

The one that appears to be favoured by most Christians is Creationism, which is the doctrine that God creates a soul, *ex nihilo* (i.e. out of nothing), for each body as and when necessary. I shall have more to say on this below.

Pre-existence is the doctrine that all souls had a prior existence before being born into mortal bodies. Jewish sources were already commenting on this, as the Wisdom of Solomon, dating to the first century BCE, attests:

> [19] As a child I was naturally gifted, and a good soul fell to my lot; [20] or rather, **being good, I entered an undefiled body.** *(Wisdom of Solomon 8:19-20 NRS.)*

We can see Paul expressing this idea in his epistle to the Ephesians:

> [4] For he [God] chose us in him **before the creation of the world** to be holy and blameless in his sight. *(Ephesians 1:4 NIV.)*

The obvious point to raise concerning pre-existence is that, if all souls were created at the same time as Adam's, it follows that they were created before he sinned! Why then should they now be in a "fallen" state? Although the doctrine of pre-existence was advance by Origen, it was condemned as heresy by the Second Council of Constantinople in 553 CE[42].

---

[42] See https://www.ccel.org/ccel/schaff/npnf214.xii.ix.html

One way some Christians found of addressing the problem of our "fallen" nature was the doctrine of **traducianism**, the *belief* that God only created Adam's soul and all other souls are *generated* from him. Traducianists claim that their doctrine is the most biblical, arguing that God finished his creative work on the sixth day, an argument that can also be used by those advocating pre-existence:

> [1] Thus the heavens and the earth were **finished,** and **all the host of them.** [2] And on the seventh day God **ended his work** which he had made; and he rested on the seventh day from **all his work** which he had made. *(Genesis 2:1-2 KJV.)*

Additionally, when God made Adam, he did not become a soul until God breathed into him the breath of life:

> [7] And the LORD God formed man *of* the dust of the ground, and breathed into his nostrils the breath of life; and man became a living soul. *(Genesis 2:7 KJV.)*

But Eve appears to come completely out of the first man, no breath of life required:

> [21] So the LORD God caused a deep sleep to fall upon the man, and he slept; then he took one of his ribs and closed up its place with flesh. [22] And the rib that the LORD God had taken from the man **he made into a woman** and brought her to the man. [23] Then the man said, "This at last is bone of my bones and flesh of my flesh; this one shall be called Woman, for out of Man this one was taken." *(Genesis 2:21-23 NRS.)*

They also refer to other passages to back up their claim, for example:

> [3] And Adam lived an hundred and thirty years, and begat *a son* in his own likeness, after his image; and called his name Seth: *(Genesis 5:3 KJV.)*

The assumption here is that "likeness" and "image" presumably includes Seth's soul.

> [11] And God said unto him [Israel], I *am* God Almighty: be fruitful and multiply; a nation and a company of nations shall be of thee, **and kings shall come out of thy loins;** *(Genesis 35:11 KJV.)*

Notice that no mention is made of any divine intervention. God appears to be implying that these kings shall come out of the body of Jacob (now named Israel) complete with both bodies and souls. Similarly,

> [9] And as I may so say, Levi also, who receiveth tithes, payed tithes in Abraham. [10] For he was **yet in the loins of his father,** when Melchisedec met him. *(Hebrews 7:9-10 KJV.)*

In asserting the superiority of the Melchisedec (more commonly Melchizedek) priesthood, the author of Hebrews is pointing out that Levi, the head of the Levitical priesthood, paid tithes *in* Abraham to Melchisedec, because he was still in the body of his ancestor Abraham when he paid tithes to Melchisedec.

Traducianists not only claim that theirs is the most biblical doctrine but that it also explains why everyone has a *fallen* nature; because, so the argument goes, when Adam sinned, everyone sinned, as we were all in the loins of Adam.

The Traducian doctrine was advocated by, amongst others, the Baptist minister and theologian Augustus H. Strong (1836–1921) in his book *Systematic Theology* and is today the prevalent view of the Lutheran Church.

We can now return to the doctrine that appears to be favoured by most Christians, i.e. Creationism. However, those maintaining that God creates each soul, *ex nihilo*, as and when necessary, still disagree as to when it is infused into a body, and this disagreement goes right to the heart of the abortion debate!

One view is that this occurs at the moment the female gamete (ovum) is fertilized. This belief is referred to as **immediate animation** (*anima* = soul). The alternative view – that the human soul was not infused at the moment of conception, but at some time between conception and birth – is usually referred to as **delayed hominization**. The change in term from animation to hominization is to make it clear that, those people believing in delayed hominization are not claiming that the zygote is not alive, only that it does not yet have a human soul.

There were two advantages in claiming delayed hominization. First, it makes a clear distinction between conception – which was caused by the parents – and ensoulment – which was initiated by God – by separating them in time.

Secondly, by this time, some prominent Christians had been influenced by the philosophy of Aristotle (384–322 BCE), a pupil of Plato. Although he always acknowledged a great debt to his mentor, Aristotle's outlook was very different. His philosophy was rooted in the natural world, especially with living things – how they came into being, grew, moved about and eventually passed away. His book *De Generatione Animalium* (On the Generation of Animals) is generally considered to mark the beginning of the history of Western embryology, and it was not until the middle of the seventeenth century that his views began to be seriously undermined by new insights on the subject.

Aristotle developed a theory of **progressive ensoulment**, where a foetus first acquires a vegetive soul, followed by an animal soul, and finally a human soul **when it is adequately developed to receive it**:

> Hence arises a question of the greatest difficulty, which we must strive to solve to the best of our ability and as far as possible. When and how and whence is a share in **reason** acquired by those animals that participate in this principle? It is plain that the semen and the embryo, while not yet separate, must be assumed to have the nutritive soul potentially, but not actually, until (like those embryos that are separated from the mother) it absorbs nourishment and performs the function of the nutritive soul. For at first **all such embryos seem to live the life of a plant**. And it is clear that we must be guided by this in speaking of the sensitive and the rational soul. **For all three kinds of soul, not only the nutritive, must be possessed**

potentially before they are possessed in actuality. *736ᵇ4-736ᵇ15⁴³*.

To fully understand his views about embryology, we need first to understand his ideas about **causes**. Aristotle insisted that a proper scientific understanding of any naturally occurring object (or, for that matter, any artificial product as well) requires an explanation of its **causes**. The Greek word for **cause** is αἴτιον (tr. aition) Unlike our generally restricted use of the term **cause**, *viz.* something producing an effect, he uses the term very broadly as *an explanation for how a thing came about*. Aristotle distinguishes four causes, which he regards as necessary for a full understanding of a *thing*; these have come to be called:

- The **material** cause – "that out of which a thing comes to be, and which persists," *viz.* the raw material(s) out of which an object is composed, e.g. gold, silver and bronze can all be the material cause of, say, a statue or chalice.
- The **formal** cause – "the account of what-it-is-to-be," *viz.* the *form* or *pattern* which makes matter into a particular thing we recognize as

---

[43] References of this type are called Bekker numbers and are based on the page numbers used in the Prussian Academy of Sciences edition of the complete works of Aristotle. They take the format of up to four numbers – to indicate page number – a letter 'a' or 'b' – to indicate the column – and the line number or numbers. Most works on Aristotle use these Bekker numbers, which take their name from August Immanuel Bekker (1785 – 1871), a German philologist who edited the above mentioned edition.

being of a certain type, e.g., the shape of the particular statue or chalice.

- The **efficient** cause – "the primary source of change or rest," *viz.* this cause is similar to the way we use the term today, e.g. the *producer* is the efficient cause of the product – the artisan who casts metal into a specific object, the doctor healing a patient and a father propagating a child.

- The **final** cause – "the end (*telos*), that for the sake of which a thing is done," *viz.* the intended purpose, aim or goal of something, e.g. a chalice could be made for use in the Eucharist or a statue may be cast in order to honour the person it represents. In addition, health, say, could be the final cause of walking, if a person is walking in order to be healthy.

When it came to human procreation, he considered the **material** cause to be the female menstrual blood. He regarded the male semen as the **efficient** cause which was required to start and guide the developing process. In his view, heredity is the result of the **form** carried by the paternal seed. If the development of the embryo proceeds perfectly successfully, then the offspring will be male, and closely resemble his father. Female offspring are the result of less perfect development and resemble their mothers!

Armed with a basic understanding of Aristotle's embryology, we can now examine his effect on Christianity.

I pointed out, in the *Introduction*, that neither St Jerome nor St Augustine viewed **all** abortion as murder. We can now see why. Both believed in delayed hominization, as the quotes below illustrate:

> The **seed** gradually takes shape in the uterus, and it [abortion] **does not count as killing** until the individual elements have acquired their external appearance and their limbs - *St. Jerome (c. 347– 419/20), letter to Algasia.*

> The law does not provide that the act (abortion) pertains to homicide, **for there cannot yet be said to be a live soul in a body that lacks sensation** when it is not formed in flesh and so is not endowed with sense. *St Augustine (354–430), On Exodus.*

Other prominent Christian theologians also believed in delayed hominization:

> **No human intellect** accepts the view that an infant has the rational soul **from the moment of conception.** *St Anselm of Canterbury (1033/34–1109.)*[44]

> He is **not a murderer** who brings about abortion **before the soul is in the body.** *Gratian*[45] *(fl. Mid-12th century), Decretals 8.32.2.*

> We must therefore say that since the generation of one thing is the corruption of another, it follows of necessity

---

[44] Quoted in *Encyclopedia of Catholicism* by Frank K. Flinn (2008) Page 4.

[45] An Italian monk who has long been acclaimed as *Pater Juris Canonici (Father of Canon Law).*

that both in men and in other animals, when a more perfect form supervenes the previous form is corrupted: yet so that the supervening form contains the perfection of the previous form, and something in addition. It is in this way that through many generations and corruptions we arrive at the ultimate substantial form, both in man and other animals. This indeed is apparent to the senses in animals generated from putrefaction. **We conclude therefore that the intellectual soul is created by God at the end of human generation**, and this soul is at the same time sensitive and nutritive, the pre-existing forms being corrupted. *St Thomas Aquinas (1224/25 – 1274), Summa Theologica: Question 118: Article 2.*

Pope Gregory XIV (1535–91) also supported the Aristotelian distinction between an "animated" and "unanimated" foetus, as the following quote shows:

In Gregory XIV's version of this [abortion] law, **the main distinction was between the foetus before and after ensoulment as defined by Aquinas**, and only the latter should be punished with excommunication. The newer version also recommended the "quickening test" **in order to establish whether or not ensoulment had taken place**. This important distinction was based on a combined theological-biological model, based on the work of Aquinas, which correlated ensoulment with the foetus' ability to move. *A History of Pregnancy in Christianity (2015) P.70.*

Quickening refers to the stage of pregnancy when the mother first feels the movements of the foetus, which generally occurs at around five months.

One question that the doctrine of creationism does not address, however is that, given God creates each soul *ex nihilo* at some time during pregnancy, why does he create them all with a "fallen" nature? After all, he is supposed, by Christians, to be omnibenevolent[46]!

When moving to contemporary debates about abortion, it is necessary to be clear about the term **conception**. Many Christians still refer to conception as occurring as soon as the sperm and the ovum unite to form a zygote. However, the scientific and medical community today generally considers conception to be when a fertilized egg (by now termed a blastocyst) has implanted itself in the wall of the uterus (a process termed nidation).

Founded in 1542 by Pope Paul III, the **Congregation for the Doctrine of the Faith** is nowadays responsible for promulgating and defending Catholic doctrine. It produced a document called *Declaration on Procured Abortion*, which was ratified by Pope Paul VI (who we encountered in Chapter 3) and delivered by him on 28 June 1974. It includes the following interesting note:

> This declaration **expressly leaves aside the question of the moment when the spiritual soul is infused**. There is not a unanimous tradition on this point **and authors are as yet in disagreement**. For some it dates from the first instant; for others it could not at least precede nidation [the implantation of an embryo in the lining of the uterus]. **It is not within the competence of science to decide between these views, because the**

---

[46] All-loving or infinitely good.

existence of an immortal soul is not a question in its field. It is a philosophical problem from which our moral affirmation remains independent for two reasons: (1) supposing a belated animation, there is still nothing less than a human life, **preparing for and calling for a soul** in which the nature received from parents is completed, (2) on the other hand, it suffices that this presence of the soul be **probable** (and **one can never prove the contrary**) in order that the taking of life involve accepting the risk of killing a man, not only waiting for, but already in possession of his soul. *Note 19.*

For those many Christians who subscribe to substance dualism, i.e. the view that humans have two parts, a physical body and an immaterial, non-physical, soul, the body is purely a material object with properties such as mass, weight and size. The soul, by contrast, has thoughts, desires, intentions and the ability for logical reasoning. That being the case, when we consider reason (1), in the above quote, it is difficult to agree with the claim that, before animation, the body is "preparing for and calling for a soul!"

I must, however, also take issue with reason (2) regarding the existence of the immortal soul, that "one can never prove the contrary," as Christians often use this type of argument against, among other things, the non-existence of God.

Whilst it is true that no one can prove that God does not exist, that does absolutely nothing to show that he does in fact exist. Likewise, with the immortal soul. This type of argument is an example of a logical fallacy called *argumentum ad ignorantiam* (argument from ignorance). In this case "ignorance" represents "a lack of contrary evidence." It is a technique often used by Christians, whilst debating, in an attempt to shift the burden of proof onto the opposing party. However, it is never the responsibility of the person denying a claim to prove otherwise. This faulty way of thinking is covered nicely by the philosopher Bertrand Russell (1872–1970) with his Celestial Teapot:

> If I were to suggest that between the Earth and Mars there is a china teapot revolving about the sun in an elliptical orbit, nobody would be able to disprove my assertion provided I were careful to add that the teapot is too small to be revealed even by our most powerful telescopes. But if I were to go on to say that, since my assertion cannot be disproved, it is an intolerable presumption on the part of human reason to doubt it, I should rightly be thought to be talking nonsense. If, however, the existence of such a teapot were affirmed in ancient books, taught as the sacred truth every Sunday, and instilled into the minds of children at school, hesitation to believe in its existence would become a mark of eccentricity and entitle the doubter to the attentions of the psychiatrist in an enlightened age or of the Inquisitor in an earlier time.

Extract from Wikipedia

Although it is obvious that science cannot disprove the existence of the immortal soul, I don't know of any scientist that would even contemplate such a futile task. You simply cannot prove such a negative. Although I don't believe in the Loch Ness Monster, the tooth fairy, or the Abominable Snowman, I cannot prove that they do not exist!

Despite its dig at "the competence of science" the Congregation is, nonetheless, quick to employ scientific findings if they agree with its own views:

> ... It [modern genetic science] has demonstrated that, from the first instant, there is established the program of what this **living being** will be: a man, **this individual man with his characteristic aspects already well determined. Right from fertilization is begun the adventure of a human life,** and each of its capacities requires time - a rather lengthy time - to find its place and to be in a position to act. *Paragraph 13.*

This paragraph continues:

> The least that can be said is that present science, in its most evolved state, does not give any substantial support to those who defend abortion. **Moreover, it is not up to biological sciences to make a definitive judgment on questions which are properly philosophical and moral such as the moment when a human person is constituted or the legitimacy of abortion**. From a moral point of view this is certain: even if a doubt existed concerning whether the fruit of conception is already a human person, it is objectively a grave sin to dare to risk murder. "The one who will be a man is already one."

What the Congregation for the Doctrine of the Faith should have realised, however, is that scientific knowledge advances and, as we have seen in areas of cosmology and evolution, scientific advances tend to *throw spanners into the works* of religion!

So, let's have a look at what modern advances in embryology tell us. It is now known that, shortly after the zygote is formed, it starts dividing to form a cluster of cells called a morula. All this normally takes place in one of the woman's fallopian

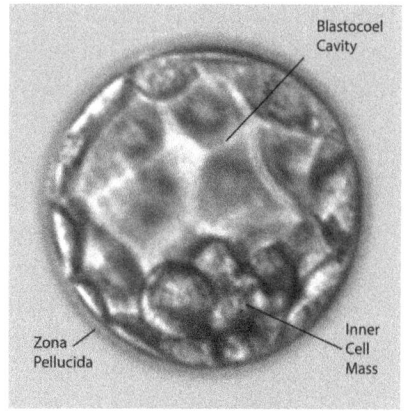

A Human Blastocyst

tubes. At around three to four days after fertilisation the morula leaves the fallopian tube and enters the uterus. At about six days after fertilisation the cluster of cells, now known as a blastocyst, burrows itself into the lining of the uterus. This process is called implantation and, as mentioned above, is the stage when the scientific and medical community generally considers conception to occur.

Now, here comes the first *spanner*!

In 2003, the German-American medical geneticist and professor at the University of Utah, John M Opitz (1935–) testified, before the American President's Council on Bioethics, that between sixty and eighty percent of all naturally conceived embryos are simply flushed out of the body, unnoticed, in women's normal menstrual flows. According to Opitz, embryologists estimate that the rate of natural loss for embryos that have developed for seven days or more is sixty percent but, if one counts from the moment of fertilization, then the total rate of natural loss increases to at least eighty percent.

You can see the problem faced by those Christians claiming that a foetus has an immortal soul, created by God, from the moment of conception (fertilisation). You have an omniscient[47] and omnipotent[48] God endowing a significant majority of foetuses with an immortal soul only to have them spontaneously abort before the woman is considered officially pregnant[49]! It would seem that nature carries out abortions at a far higher rate than any human society. So, we can see that the claim made by many anti-abortionists that, left undisturbed, most zygotes will go on to become persons, is simply not true!

A second *spanner* came to light even earlier – identical twins. Although most twins are formed when the blastocyst and its inner cell mass *hatches* out of the zona pellucida[50], they can be formed at any time from conception up to day fourteen. So, if God endows souls

---

[47] All-knowing; infinitely wise.

[48] All-powerful.

[49] Here I am using the scientific and medical communities commonly held view that a woman is considered pregnant only when a fertilized egg has implanted in the wall of her uterus.

[50] The membrane that forms around an ovum as it develops in the ovary. If fertilization takes place, it disappears to permit implantation in the uterus.

at the moment of conception, what happens in the case of twins that form sometime later? Which **identical** twin, for example, gets the original soul?

Contrary to the statement above, by the Congregation for the Doctrine of the Faith, that:

> ... It [modern genetic science] has demonstrated that, from the first instant, there is established the program of what this **living being** will be: a man, **this individual man with his characteristic aspects already well determined. Right from fertilization is begun the adventure of a human life** ...

the occurrence of identical twinning indicates that logically this cannot be the case. Granted that one's genetic, or biological, identity is established at the zygote stage, nevertheless, that clearly does not imply that one's ontological identity is established at the same time. If a zygote has the capacity to develop into two ontologically distinct human individuals, then how could it possibly be regarded as one distinct individual with a its own soul?

Hence, rather than demonstrating that "from the first instant" there is an "individual man with his characteristic aspects already well determined", modern genetic science appears to throw considerable doubt on this claim! In fact, many bioethicists consider that experimentation with human embryos is permissible before the **primitive streak**[51] develops at around the fourteenth day after

---

[51] The primitive streak is a structure that forms in the blastocyst during the early stages of embryonic development.

fertilization. They take the development of the primitive streak as signifying the creation of a unique human being and, in Britain as well as some other countries, it is permissible to develop a human embryo for up to 14 days outside a woman's body.

Thus far, our examination of the Christian concept of the immortal soul has shown that it came from Greek philosophy and, with no Scripture to refer to, disagreements have raged about it up to the present day, even within Christianity itself. So, with no way to prove the existence, or non-existence, of immortal souls, unless we wish to blindly follow those *authorities* that propound such a view, we must fall back on our own judgement.

We can summarise the Catholic and evangelical Protestant view as:

> There is an omnibenevolent, omniscient, and omnipotent God who creates an immortal soul, *ex nihilo*, every time an ovum is fertilized, and then infuses it into the resulting zygote. Consequently, there exists, from the moment of fertilization, a unique and complete person that has the same right to life as any other person, in particular, the woman in whose body it is developing.

The question is: Does this *belief*, or *opinion*, stand up to scrutiny? I would proffer the following points:

- According to embryologists, a majority of fertilized ova spontaneously abort prior to implantation. So, you have an omniscient and omnipotent God creating a majority of persons, only to have them abort before the woman is considered officially pregnant. A significant number of foetuses also spontaneously abort after implantation. Consequently, it is estimated that only about 30% of zygotes actually result in a live birth! God would, therefore, seem to have a very casual attitude to human lives.

- This *belief*, or *opinion*, would also have an omnibenevolent God endorsing new persons being conceived as a result of rape and incest, as well as in the event of contraception failure. I would argue that a God that caused such anxiety and distress would be hard to admire, let alone worship!

- If a unique and complete person is claimed to exist from the moment of fertilization, then the occurrence of twinning, up to fourteen days after that moment, would need to be satisfactorily explained.

- If souls are immortal, if follows that abortion will not kill them!

With the exception of twinning, the above points also apply to those Christians who agree with such luminaries as St Jerome, St Augustine, St Anselm, Gratian, St Thomas Aquinas and Pope Gregory XIV, among others, that an immortal soul does not enter the body until around the time of *quickening* (i.e. at about five months gestation)

It is worth pointing out here that, according to the latest figures published by the Department of Health and

Social Care, for England and Wales for 2019, less than 2% of legal abortions were carried out later than 19 weeks gestation and over 91% were carried out within 12 weeks or less. Legal abortions carried out where the gestation was 24[52] weeks or over, the point at which the foetus is considered as viable outside the mother's body, was 0.1% of the total.

In this chapter, we have considered the dualist view of human ontology. Even if this view is correct, we have seen that many prominent Christians, including saints, do not regard a foetus as achieving a *right to life* until well after most abortions have taken place.

Although the majority Christian belief is that a *human being* is constituted of a material body and an immaterial soul, it has always faced the seemingly intractable problem of how these two radically different kinds of substance can work together with one another. *Soul-stuff* allegedly has none of the properties of *material-stuff*, and so where and how do they interact with each other?

Advances in various branches of science have seriously begun to challenge this dualistic ontology as the following quote illustrates:

> Recent rapid advances in the study of the human brain within neuroscience, neuropsychology, and clinical neurology are making it **increasingly hard to find a realm of human thought, decision, action, or experience that is not the product of, or very strongly influenced**

---

[52] The legal limit for abortion unless the mother's life is at risk or the child would be born severely disabled.

by, the activity of identifiable neural systems. Thus, there seems to be a rapidly diminishing pool of human capacities and experiences that have not yet been found to be influenced by neural activity and that might be reserved for the activity of an ontologically distinct and immaterial soul. **Research in neuroscience raises the possibility that the concept of a separate, immaterial soul is unnecessary with respect to understanding human life and experience. Unless the soul can be shown to have a separate and identifiable realm of agency, the concept adds nothing critical to understanding humanness.** *Neurological Embodiment of Spirituality and Soul. In From Cells to Souls - and beyond: Changing Portraits of Human Nature P.59.*

Today the prevailing view held in much of western science is that of **Reductive Physicalism**, a doctrine that states that, in general, everything in the world can be reduced to its fundamental physical, or material, basis. When it comes to human beings, this doctrine holds that a person's thoughts, feelings, sensations, etc. are seen as issuing from certain chemical and biological components of a person's physiological makeup. This idea is behind, for example, psychiatrists prescribing anti-depressants to a patient, *viz.* change the patient's brain chemistry and you change the patient's mood.

This is not the place to delve further into human ontology[53], I merely want to show, at this stage, that there are different plausible opinions as to what, ontologically, a *human being* is.

---

[53] It has been claimed that there are as many as 130 different views of human ontology.

Chapter 5

Ethics and Abortion

Man is the measure of all things. Of the things that *are*, that they *are*. Of the things that *are not*, that they *are not*. Protagoras (c. 490–c.420 BCE) Greek Sophist.

In the previous chapter, I introduced the distinction between the term's *human being* and *person*. The reason being was to enable us to separate the scientifically *factual* components of an entity from any moral *value* or *legal status* that it might have. This is because, at the heart of the abortion argument is the question whether the human foetus is rightly considered a *person* in the moral or legal, *rights-holding* sense.

This distinction is particularly relevant for the abortion debate in America, as Section 1 of the 14th Amendment to the US Constitution states the following:

> All **persons** born or naturalized in the United States, and subject to the jurisdiction thereof, are **citizens** of the United States and of the State wherein they reside. No State shall make or enforce any law which shall abridge the privileges or immunities of **citizens** of the United States; nor shall any State deprive any **person of** life, liberty, or property, without due process of law; **nor deny to any person within its jurisdiction the equal protection of the laws.**

It, therefore, follows that if foetuses are *persons* under the Constitution, then abortions would be illegal. This was specifically stated in the landmark Supreme Court case of Roe v. Wade in 1973:

> The appellee and certain amici argue that the fetus is a "person" within the language and meaning of the Fourteenth Amendment. In support of this, they outline at length and in detail the well-known facts of fetal development. If this suggestion of personhood is established, the appellant's case, of course, collapses, [410 U.S. 113, 157] **for the fetus' right to life would then be guaranteed specifically by the Amendment.**

However, the Supreme Court decision acknowledges that "The Constitution does not define 'person' in so many words" and goes on to state that:

> All this, together with our observation, supra, that throughout the major portion of the 19th century prevailing legal abortion practices were far freer than they are today, **persuades us that the word "person," as used in the Fourteenth Amendment, does not include the unborn.**

Further, it goes on to declare that:

> Texas urges that, apart from the Fourteenth Amendment, life begins at conception and is present throughout pregnancy, and that, therefore, the State has a compelling interest in protecting that life from and after conception. We need not resolve the difficult question of **when life begins. When those trained in the respective disciplines of medicine, philosophy, and**

theology are unable to arrive at any consensus, the judiciary, at this point in the development of man's knowledge, is not in a position to speculate as to the answer.

Although this passage talks about 'when life begins,' it is patently talking about 'life' in the moral and legal sense, which we are referring to as *personhood*, rather than the biological sense. It is worth bearing in mind, however, that because the Roe v. Wade decision allowed for abortion, *effectively* on demand, the Supreme Court of the US did not consider a foetus to be a person under the Constitution!

But why are doctors, philosophers, and theologians "unable to arrive at any consensus" on this issue? A large part of the problem concerns being able to define the term *personhood* universally. What is it that makes individuals, like you and me, *persons* with the moral and legal *rights* that we possess? Before we look specifically at this issue, we need some familiarity with the subject of ethics in general, as it is not clear that even if a foetus is awarded the status of personhood, then abortion is morally wrong!

Leaving aside descriptive moral philosophy[54], which sets out to investigate and report on *what* individuals or groups actually do, and what moral standards they claim to adhere to, the field of moral philosophy is usually divided into three general subject areas: metaethics, normative ethics and applied ethics.

---

[54] Also known as comparative ethics.

Applied ethics relates directly to the examination of specific, often controversial, topics. "Should we bring back capital punishment?" "Should we allow same sex marriage?" and "Is abortion wrong?" are all examples of specific questions dealt with in applied ethics. More generally, applied ethics asks questions like: "What is the right thing to do, given this specific situation?"

However, in order to answer the questions raised in applied ethics, relying on intuition, gut reaction or even tradition are far from satisfactory ways of proceeding. For example, female circumcision[55] is a common practice in several countries, some of which regard it as a social norm. Justifications given for the practice include religious necessity/approval, social acceptance and better marriage prospects. Anyone wishing to condemn this custom on ethical grounds needs to provide rational arguments using established **principles**. It is the role of **normative ethics** to try to establish such principles and to arrive at moral standards (or norms) and systems that tell us right from wrong. For example, the **Divine Command Theory** and **Natural Law Theory**, considered below, are examples of normative systems.

Nevertheless, all of our beliefs rest on some basic, *assumed*, beliefs and ethical theories are no exception; they all have some kind of starting, or **grounding**, *assumptions*. It is these *assumptions* that are, among other things, the subject of **metaethics**. In general,

---

[55] Usually referred to as Female Genital Mutilation (FGM) in the Western world. Notice the negative moral connotation here which does not generally accompany male circumcision!

metaethics can be described as the study of ethical systems, especially regarding their key concepts, techniques of analysis and linguistic conventions. Are there moral *facts*? If there are moral facts, what is their origin? Are moral standards universal or relative? How are terms such as *good*, *bad*, *right,* and *wrong* to be defined? These are the sorts of questions that metaethics attempts to answer.

For those new to ethics, it is worth bearing in mind that it is not like a discipline in science like, say, physics, where there is a large body of accepted 'truth' that beginners are expected to master. Granted, there are still some unresolved controversies in physics, but these take place against a large area of consensus. Newcomers to physics would not be asked, for example, to make up their own minds about the laws of motion. In ethics, by contrast, virtually everything is disputed even, as we shall discover, down to the basics, and newcomers will need to make up their own minds between contested theories.

One *tool* that ethicists frequently employ, when trying to extract and test **moral principles,** is the **thought experiment**. One famous thought experiment – *The Runaway Trolley* – will illustrate some of the subtleties that ethicists are required to address:

> Suppose you are the driver of a trolley car hurtling down the track at considerable speed. Up ahead you see five workers standing on the track. You try to stop but the brakes don't work. You feel desperate because you know that if you crash into these five workers,

they will all die (in this hypothetical case, you know that for sure). Suddenly, you notice a side track, off to the right, with a single worker on it. You realize that you can turn the trolley car onto the side track, killing the one worker but sparing the five. What would you do and why?

Almost unanimously, people presented with this situation, say that they would turn the trolley car onto the side track, reasoning that killing one innocent person is better than killing five innocent people.

This type of ethical reasoning is known as **Consequentialism**, which maintains that our actions are right or wrong because, and *only because*, of their consequences. The *only because* is important here as almost all modern ethical theories take consequences into account to some degree or another. What distinguishes the consequentialist from the non-consequentialist is their insistence that, when it comes to rightness and wrongness, nothing matters but the results of our actions.

To someone new to the study of ethics, this seems a reasonable position to adopt, until they are confronted by a slightly different *Runaway Trolley* scenario:

In this situation, you are not the driver but an onlooker, standing on a bridge overlooking a track with five workers on it. This time there is no side track. The trolley car is about to crash into the five workers, and you feel helpless to avert this disaster, until you notice a very fat man leaning over the bridge directly above the track. You could give him a push and he would fall off the bridge directly into the path of the trolley car, killing him but the five workers would be saved. Being virtuous, you had considered jumping onto the track yourself, but you realized that you are not big enough to stop the trolley car. Do you push the fat man?

Virtually all the people who would turn the trolley car onto the side track, in the first example, would not push the fat man off the bridge, considering it morally wrong to do so. So, the obvious question is, what happened to the **principle** that killing one innocent person is better than killing five innocent people?

These different versions of the *Runaway Trolley* bring two moral principles – i.e. *better to kill one innocent person in order to save five*, and, *it is wrong to kill an innocent person, even for a good cause* – into direct conflict. What happens if killing one innocent person does not save just five, but five hundred or five thousand! Where and when does a person's *right to life* give way to the good of society as a whole, if it ever does?

It is problems like this where moral disagreements persist even to this day. What is important for us to accept is that, even given exactly the same facts, different people will often make different choices whilst *believing* that they are doing the morally right thing. Life in a democratic, multi-cultural society is rife with disagreements about right and wrong, justice and injustice.

As we can see, from the quote under the heading, Protagoras argued that moral rules were merely conventions created by society, with different societies adopting different rules. We see this in our current time, with different attitudes to, for example, female circumcision and abortion. This is known as **moral relativism** and is the opposite of **moral absolutism**. For moral absolutists some things are always right, and some things are always wrong, no matter what culture or society you belong to. They argue that it is possible to find some basic feature upon which a system of ethics can be built. Once that foundation is established, moral principles, the right or wrong of particular actions, and the truth or falsity of moral *propositions* can be ascertained by logical deduction.

Let's examine how this is usually applied to our topic of abortion.

In philosophy, the technical term for a statement that is either true or false is a *proposition*, and to say that a statement is *truth-apt* is to say that it could be uttered in some context (without its meaning being altered) and would then express a true or false proposition, *viz.* truth-apt sentences unlike, say, questions, prescriptions or commands, are capable of being true or false.

Now, consider the statement:

Abortion is wrong.

Can this statement actually be true or false? **Cognitivists** answer "yes" to this question, regarding such an assertion as being as *factual* as statements such as 'Albert Einstein was a physicist', 'It's raining outside' and 'The moon is made of cheese.' On the other hand,

Noncognitivists would answer 'no' to this question, claiming that such an assertion is expressing a non-belief state, such as an emotion. For example, it may simply be expressing a disapproval of abortion ("boo abortion"), or a command not to abort ("don't abort").

Most anti-abortionists would take the cognitivist stance, claiming that "Abortion is wrong" is a statement that is, not only truth-apt, but actually true. So, if we *assume*, for the moment, that they are right. The next, obvious, question becomes:

Is wrongness an objective,
mind-independent property?

Moral Realists will claim that it is. They claim that moral values are features of the world no less real than, say, gravity or solidity. **Moral Subjectivists**, on the other hand, would answer "no", claiming that the statement "Abortion is wrong" simply means that "I disapprove of abortion" (**Individualist subjectivism**) or "My culture disapproves of abortion" (**Cultural subjectivism**).

Once again, most anti-abortionists take the realist stance, claiming that when they state that "abortion is wrong" they are making a true statement about an objective, mind-independent fact.

Again, *assuming*, for the sake of argument, that they are right, we can now legitimately ask:

Where do these objective, mind-independent
properties come from?

Many Christians will confidently claim, at this stage, that they come from God. In fact, they often go further by stating that, without God, there would be no reason to act morally. We have now arrived at the first normative theory that I want to examine – the **Divine Command Theory** – but bear in mind how many *assumptions* we needed to make just to get here!

The Divine Command Theory is the oldest and most widely held ethical theory in the world; espoused by both some monotheistic and polytheistic cultures. Put simply, this theory declares that what is moral is determined by God, and that to be moral is to follows God's commands. Normativity, therefore, depends on God's **will** and, thus, gets its **authority** outside of human nature. Hence, it follows that moral truth does not exist independently of God. This is why many Christians, misquoting the Russian novelist Fyodor Dostoyevsky (1821–81), claim that "If there is no God, everything is permitted." In other words, if God did not exist, then nothing would be right or wrong and people would be free to do as they please, including murdering and rape.

One argument put forward in favour of this theory is that, if God created the universe *ex nihilo*[56], then it follows that **everything** in it, including our understanding of right and wrong comes from God.

However, in Plato's dialogue Euthyphro, Socrates asks the question "Is the pious loved by the gods because it is

---

[56] Latin "out of nothing".

pious, or is it pious because it is loved by the gods?" This question has given rise to what is called the **Euthyphro Dilemma,** eloquently presented by Wilhelm Gottfried Leibniz (1646–1716), a German philosopher and mathematician:

> It is generally agreed that whatever God wills is good and just. But there remains the question whether it is good and just because God wills it or whether God wills it because it is good and just; in other words, whether justice and goodness are **arbitrary** or whether they belong to **the necessary and eternal truths about the nature of things**.

Now, a dilemma is a situation in which you are forced to choose between two options, both of which lead to unpleasant results. Philosophers have likened a dilemma to holding an angry bull by the horns, and so the two unpleasant options are known as *horns*.

One *horn* – that which is good and just is commanded by God simply because it is good and just – is the one that most religionists wish to avoid, as it leads to some conclusions which they find unpalatable:

- If moral standards exist independently of God, and he commands a particular action because it is morally right, then ethics no longer depend on God in the way that the Divine Command Theory upholds. In addition, both moral and immoral acts would retain their character even if God did not exist.
- If moral standards are independent of God, then there is something over which God is not

sovereign and, what's more, God's goodness would depend on the extent to which he complied with these autonomously existing moral standards. This would, therefore, also place restrictions on any claims of God's omnipotence.

- If the ethical rules of the universe come from some source other than God, then why can't we just go straight to that source too, and figure out morality for ourselves, in the same way that God did?

The other *horn* – that which is good and just is good and just because it is commanded by God – is most synonymous with the Divine Command Theory. However, this *horn* also leads to some conclusions which many find unacceptable:

- Equating goodness with God's commands means that statements like "God is good" and "God's commands are good" become meaningless or tautological. In effect they are just saying that "God acts in accordance with his commands" and "God's commands are in accordance with his commands".

- As Leibniz presentation points out, if there are no moral standards independent of God's will, then God's commands are arbitrary and not based on reason! How could such arbitrary commands form the foundation of morality? In his *Discourse on Metaphysics* he states:

> In saying, therefore, that things are not good according to any standard of goodness, but simply

by the will of God, it seems to me that one destroys, without realizing it, all the love of God and all his glory; **for why praise him for what he has done, if he would be equally praiseworthy in doing the contrary?** Where will be his justice and his wisdom if he has only a certain despotic power, **if arbitrary will takes the place of reasonableness**, and if in accord with the definition of tyrants, justice consists in that which is pleasing to the most powerful?

- Such arbitrariness would mean that anything could become good merely because God commands it. For example, if God commanded us to inflict suffering on others, then doing so would become the morally right thing to do.

Some Christians try to claim that the dilemma is irrelevant by arguing that God's commands cannot be arbitrary; although God could theoretically command things like, for example, murder, theft, and rape, he would not do so because that is not in his nature. In other words, saying that "God is good" is similar to claiming that "Bachelors are unmarried males"; both are truisms.

However, reading through the Old Testament, you will not only come across such seemingly arbitrary prohibitions against, say, tattooing[57], wearing clothes made of wool and linen woven together[58], and cooking

---

[57] Leviticus 19:28.
[58] Deuteronomy 22:11.

a young goat in its mother's milk[59], but also the death penalty as punishment for, among other things, cursing your father or mother[60] and for working on the Sabbath[61] (firemen, nurses, bus drivers, etc. take note!). More seriously though, consider the following passages:

> [16] But as for the towns of these peoples that the LORD your God is giving you as an inheritance, you must not let anything that breathes remain alive. [17] You shall annihilate them-- the Hittites and the Amorites, the Canaanites and the Perizzites, the Hivites and the Jebusites-- just as the LORD your God has commanded, *(Deuteronomy 20:16-17 NRS.)*

> [1] Samuel said to Saul, "The LORD sent me to anoint you king over his people Israel; now therefore listen to the words of the LORD. [2] Thus says the LORD of hosts, 'I will punish the Amalekites for what they did in opposing the Israelites when they came up out of Egypt. [3] Now go and attack Amalek, and utterly destroy all that they have; do not spare them, **but kill both man and woman, child and infant,** ox and sheep, camel and donkey.'" *(1Samuel 15:1-3 NRS.)*

Here we have the God of all three monotheistic religions commanding genocide[62]. What he had against the Amalekite's ox, sheep, camels, and donkeys is another

---

[59] Exodus 34:26.

[60] Exodus 21:17.

[61] Exodus 31:15.

[62] The term is derived from the Greek *genos* = 'race', 'tribe' or 'nation' + the Latin *cide* = 'killing'; and is the deliberate and systematic extermination of a national, racial, political or cultural group.

question entirely! Now, modern international law considers genocide a "crime against humanity" and I think that anyone with a correctly functioning moral compass would consider the intentional slaughter of innocent women and children as immoral.

Next consider the following:

> [44] As for your male and female slaves who may belong to you– you may buy male and female slaves from the nations all around you. [45] Also you may buy slaves from the children of the foreigners who reside with you, and from their families that are with you, whom they have fathered in your land, **they may become your property**. [46] You may give them as inheritance to your children after you **to possess as property. You may enslave them perpetually**. However, as for your brothers the Israelites, no man may rule over his brother harshly. *(Leviticus 25:44-46 NET.)*

Here we have this same God not only condoning slavery but giving instructions on where the Israelites should get their slaves from, i.e. non-Israelites!

For Christians objecting to the fact that this is the Old Testament, which is no longer relevant since Christ came along, notice that Jesus, who they claim is also God, condoned flogging slaves as well:

> [47] That slave who knew what his master wanted, but did not prepare himself or do what was wanted, will receive a severe beating. [48] But the one who did not know and did what deserved a beating will receive a light beating. *(Luke 12:47-48 NRS.)*

It follows, therefore, that he had no moral qualms against people owning them! So, for anyone who considers genocide and slavery to be morally wrong, the Divine Command Theory appears to have serious shortcomings – just because God, according to scripture, commands or condones a particular action, for many people that does not make it morally justifiable. It may have taken some time, but civilised societies have developed moral codes, and associated laws, **despite the Bible** and not because of it.

Notwithstanding the evidence from the Bible, many Christians will adamantly insist that God is good. This being the case, it is legitimate to ask them what the basis for their *belief* is. If they claim that the Bible, taken as a whole, teaches this, or that Jesus embodied and displayed God's goodness, then it can be pointed out that the believer must have some logically prior, and independent, criterion of goodness, based on something apart from the fact that God exists; otherwise, how do they know that their beliefs about the Bible or Jesus support their belief that God is good? In other words, you need to know what 'goodness' is **before** you can judge the goodness of God from the Bible or Jesus.

Given the obvious problems with the Divine Command Theory, many theists turn to another normative theory – **Natural Law Theory**. We saw Pope Paul VI refer to "the natural law" in his encyclical *Humanae Vitae*, in Chapter 3, and many Catholic ethical precepts are rooted in this normative theory.

There are several versions of this theory circulating around today – some not even relying on belief in God – but the most influential and long-standing version is that espoused by the Italian Dominican theologian Thomas Aquinas (1224/25–74).

Put simply, this theory holds that God created the universe in such a way that the laws of morality are actually *embedded* into it, much like the laws of physics and, being made in the "image of God," man can discover these laws by the use of his reason.

Aquinas was strongly influenced by the philosophy of Aristotle who, among other things, was the first to write an actual treatise on ethics. Many people regard him as the *father* of natural law. In Chapter 4, I explained Aristotle's four causes, and natural law is strongly connected with his final cause – "the end (*telos*), that for the sake of which a thing is done." For Aristotle nature makes nothing without a purpose, and all her processes aim at some end. He even states that *purpose* (literally "that for the sake of which") is more evident in the works of nature than in those of human art:

> Furthermore, the causes concerned in natural generation are, as we see, more than one. There is the cause *for the sake of which*, and the cause whence the beginning of motion comes. Now we must decide which of these two causes comes first, which second. Plainly, however, that cause is the first which we call *that for the sake of which*. For this is the account of the thing, and the account forms the starting-point, alike in the works of art and the works of nature. For the doctor and the builder define health or house, either by

the intellect or by perception, and then proceed to give the accounts and the causes of each of the things they do and of why they should do it thus. Now in the works of nature the good and *that for the sake of which* is still more dominant than in works of art. *639^{b}11ff*

For Aristotle, not only does everything have a function and purpose, but its highest *good* is found when it fulfils that purpose to its best capability. To give a simple example, the function of a knife is to cut and, therefore, its highest *good* would be when it was sharp and cut easily and cleanly. He argues that the human function is rational activity, and the ultimate human goal is *eudaimonia*[63]. To answer the question of how to achieve *eudaimonia*, he introduces another important concept in Greek moral philosophy, namely *arete*[64]. So, for Aristotle, human *good* is achieved when we use our rationality to the best of our abilities.

It should be noted that for Aristotle the universe was eternal and, therefore, did not have a cause, *viz.* there was no creator god. In addition, his god – the "Unmoved Mover" – was not in any way concerned with the cosmos, let alone mankind.

So, for Aquinas to incorporate Natural Law into Christianity he needed to make some modifications. For

---

[63] *Eudaimonia* (Gk. *eu* = "good" + *daimōn* = "spirit") is commonly translated as 'happiness' but is better understood as 'human flourishing' or 'fulfilment'.

[64] *Arete* is commonly translated as 'virtue', but in its general sense means 'excellence of any kind'.

him Natural Law was an extension of the **Eternal Law** – the principles by which God created and controls the universe – *viz*. it is participation in the Eternal Law by rational creatures that is called the Natural Law. Aquinas argued that we have been *designed* by God to pursue 'good' and, therefore, the starting point for Natural Law is the **Synderesis**[65] **Rule** – "that good is to be done and pursued, and evil is to be avoided"; all other precepts of the Natural Law are based upon this. He went on to identity **primary precepts** or primary 'goods' which can be discovered by observing natural human tendencies and then using our reason.

These five primary precepts are:

- to worship God
- to preserve life and defend the innocent
- to live peacefully in a well-ordered society
- to reproduce
- to nurture and educate the young and to learn.

Although these primary precepts are **absolute** and **universal**, applying to everyone without exception, they are very general and do not tell us exactly how to act in any specific situation. However, **secondary precepts**, which could be deduced from the primary precepts, are more specific and can be applied to practical situations. For example, from the primary precept to live peacefully in a well-ordered society, we could deduce the secondary precept "Do not steal," as it destroys the trust on which

---

[65] Also called Synteresis.

a well-ordered society functions; and from the primary precept to reproduce, we get the secondary precepts "Do not use contraception" and "Do not procure an abortion."

It is important to realise, however, that these secondary precepts are dependent on our own judgements, which can be open to faulty reasoning and may consequently lead to wrong choices. For example, the primary precepts, being absolutist, tend to lead to equally inflexible secondary precepts. Since at least the fourth century, the Roman Catholic Church had been opposed to all forms of contraception, and it was not until 2010 that Pope Benedict XVI ended the ban on the use of condoms, provided that the sole intention for their use was to reduce the risk of infection from Aids.

However, more fundamental criticisms of Natural Law Theory have been made, including:

- It commits the **naturalist fallacy**, by attempting to move from the *facts* about the essential nature of the world to *values* about how we *ought* to live in it. For example, it is natural for someone who is seriously ill, or injured, to die. Does that mean that health care professionals should not intervene in an attempt to save them? Also, in the natural world, the strongest members of a species usually mate with as many sexual partners as they can, often fighting off, and sometimes killing, weaker rivals. Does that mean that monogamy *ought* to be abandoned and replaced by selective breeding?

- The claim that nature is purposive and goal-oriented has been, at the very least, seriously undermined by Charles Darwin's theory of natural selection.

In order to get to both the Divine Command Theory and the Natural Law Theory, we *assumed*, for the sake of argument, the **cognitivist** and **moral realist** positions. However, many ethicists take issue with these assumptions. Exploring other normative theories is beyond the scope of this book, as I only needed to explain the problems with the two described above.

In contrast to consequentialist theories, the Divine Command Theory and the Natural Law Theory are **deontological**. Deontological ethics (from the Greek "*deon*" = "duty" or "obligation") focus on the rightness or wrongness of an action, *viz.* actions are considered good, or bad, owing to some *innate* characteristic of the action itself. The maxim *Fiat justitia ruat caelum* ("Let justice be done though the heavens fall") would be a simple descriptive expression of this principle. Clearly, the Divine Command Theory is deontological because anyone advocating it has a duty to follow God's commands. Natural Law Theory is also considered deontological because the secondary precepts generally lead to a set of rules that people have a duty to follow.

One command in the Bible is "You shall not kill[66] (Exodus 20:13 and Deuteronomy 5:17). In the original

---

[66] Often translated as "murder".

Hebrew, this command does not prohibit capital punishment or the killing of Israel's enemies during war. It does, however, specifically forbid the wilful killing of the *innocent*. Also, one of Natural Law's primary precepts was listed as "to preserve life and defend the innocent."

So, imagine that you are the Minister of Defence of a country, and you are informed that a civilian passenger plane has been hijacked with three-hundred passengers on board. The plane is heading towards your capital city and intelligence suggests that the intent of the hijackers is to crash the plane into one of the city's skyscrapers, with the objective of killing as many people as possible. Attempts to negotiate with the hijackers, or to divert the plane, have all been unsuccessful and time is now running out – you cannot evacuate the skyscraper in time. Assuming you had the authority to do so, would you order the plane to be shot down?

Well, as a response to the terrorist attacks of 11 September 2001 in the USA, the Aviation Security Act (Luftsicherheitsgesetz) was brought into effect in Germany in January 2005; Section 14.3 of which gave the Minister of Defence permission to order the shooting down of a plane in such circumstances.

However, in February 2006, the German Federal Constitutional Court[67] struck down Section 14.3, declaring it void, on the grounds that it violated the

---

[67] The supreme constitutional court.

"human dignity" and "inalienable rights" of the passengers and crew on board the aircraft. Germany has a constitution, the first 2 articles of which state:

Article 1

(1) Human dignity shall be inviolable. To respect and protect it shall be the duty of all state authority.

(2) The German people therefore acknowledge inviolable and inalienable human rights as the basis of every community, of peace and of justice in the world.

(3) The following basic rights shall bind the legislature, the executive and the judiciary as directly applicable law.

Article 2

(1) Every person shall have the right to free development of his personality insofar as he does not violate the rights of others or offend against the constitutional order or the moral law.

(2) Every person shall have the right to life and physical integrity. Freedom of the person shall be inviolable. These rights may be interfered with only pursuant to a law.

Because of the inviolable and inalienable human rights accorded to each passenger and crewman, the *consequences* of not shooting down the plane – including the almost certain death of those passengers and crewmen – become, in effect, irrelevant. It is not surprising that many people consider this as nonsensical. Not giving any consideration to the *consequences* of an action (or in this case inaction) would appear to be a serious omission.

Consider, also, the case of Magnus Gäfgen, a German law student, who on 27 September 2002 kidnapped Jakob von Metzler, the 11-year-old son of a prominent Frankfurt banker, demanding €1,000,000 ransom.

Gäfgen was observed by the police when he picked up the ransom and arrested. Believing that Jakob might still be alive Wolfgang Daschner, the deputy police chief at the time, ordered the interrogating officer to threaten Gäfgen with torture. The threat worked and Gäfgen confessed that he had killed the boy and revealed where the body was hidden. The following year, Gäfgen was convicted of murder and sentenced to life imprisonment.

What is controversial about the case is that in December 2004 Daschner received a suspended sentence of a €10,800 fine for ordering the subordinate to threaten Gäfgen with torture, and the subordinate was sentenced to a €3,600 fine. Both were dismissed from their posts. Subsequently, in August 2011 Gäfgen was awarded €3,000 damages for the police threat to torture him.

Now, if you would be prepared to give an order to shoot down a plane hijacked by terrorists or consider the interrogation technique used against Gäfgen to be morally permissible, then you must accept that some human *rights* are not inviolable or inalienable, and this is one major area of disagreement in ethical debates. So, what are these *rights* and where do they come from?

It turns out that they are not *things* (i.e. objects) that exist ontologically in the external world. Instead, they are *entitlements* or *just claims* that originate from moral theories or legal rules. An analogy should make this clear.

British law is predicated on the *presumption of innocence*. When a person is charged with a crime, they are deemed to be innocent until proven guilty. In reality however a guilty person is guilty long before that, i.e. from the moment they commit the crime. Nevertheless, although this is *actually* the case, it makes more sense to talk about such people as though they really are innocent until proven guilty; not because it is *objectively* true, but because it is considered to lead to a better legal system.

In a similar way, it makes sense to have a conception of *rights*, not because they ontologically exist, but because doing so leads to better moral and legal systems. So, although they don't actually exist themselves, *rights* are simply a useful means by which to apply moral ideas. They are then often given authority by both international and national legislative bodies.

The concept of *rights* first appeared on the international agenda with the United Nations Charter in 1945, which declared, among other things "to reaffirm faith in fundamental human rights, in the dignity and worth of the **human person**, in the equal rights of men and women and of nations large and small." In 1948 the United Nations General Assembly proclaimed the Universal Declaration of Human Rights (UDHR), which is still considered as a milestone document in the history of human rights. Article 1 of the UDHR states:

> All human beings are born free and equal in dignity and rights. They are endowed with reason and conscience and should act towards one another in a spirit of brotherhood.

And Article 3 states:

> Everyone has the **right to life**, liberty and the security of **person**.

The impression given is that *rights* are conferred on *persons* – i.e. beings endowed with reason and conscience, capable of acting in a spirit of brotherhood with each other. We can now see the advantage of making a distinction between *human beings* and *persons*, i.e. a member of the species *homo sapiens* is a *human being* – end of story. However, from a moral and legal point of view, they can acquire and lose *personhood*. Consider the following case:

> On 22 July 2011 Anders Behring Breivik, a Norwegian right-wing extremist, killed eight people by detonating a bomb in Norway's capital city, Oslo, and then killed 69 people in a summer camp on the island of Utoya.

Clearly, Breivik is a *human being*, a fact that no one can take away from him. However, he is also a *moral agent*, someone who can be held accountable for his actions. If we attribute *rights* to *persons,* as opposed to *human beings*, then we can make a judgement as to whether he has lost his *right to life* and, if so, consider whether capital punishment would be a suitable penalty for his crimes. That, however, is a debate that will have to be left for another time.

The question concerning us, however, is not if, or when, a *person* can lose *personhood*, but when does a *human being* acquire it?

The Christian Institute, and other groups opposed to abortion, claim that human personhood begins at conception. They argue that other proposed thresholds such as, for example, quickening, viability, birth, consciousness, and rationality are, unlike conception, arbitrary.

Before we examine this claim, it is worth recognizing that there are two views on the acquisition of *personhood*, *viz*. **Punctualism** and **Gradualism**.

Punctualism is the belief that a *human being* acquires *personhood* wholly and instantaneously at some given moment during gestation. The expression 'existential pop' coined by the late moral philosopher Warren Quinn, gets the idea across nicely. Gradualism, on the other hand, contradicts this idea and claims instead that *personhood* is acquired gradually and incrementally.

We can see how anyone believing that we are a human body animated by an immortal and immaterial soul, which is created by God *ex nihilo* and infused into us at conception, would be attracted to the punctualist viewpoint.

Although they can, obviously, offer no proof for their claim, they argue that, since any proposed threshold of personhood must be accompanied by an account of what constitutes ethical personhood in universal terms, all other thresholds suffer from being arbitrary. Without detailing their objections to all of the other proposed thresholds, we can just examine two of the most commonly suggested ones, i.e. viability and birth.

A foetus is considered viable when it is potentially able to live outside the mother's womb, albeit with artificial aid. The logic for using this as a legal threshold is clearly stated in the Roe v. Wade case mentioned above:

> With respect to the State's important and legitimate interest in **potential life, the "compelling" point is at viability**. This is so because the fetus then presumably **has the capability of meaningful life outside the mother's womb**. State regulation protective of fetal life after viability thus **has both logical and biological justifications**. If the State is interested in protecting fetal life after viability, it may go so far as to proscribe abortion [410 U.S. 113, 164] during that period, except when it is necessary to preserve the life or health of the mother.

Two problems with this particular threshold are:

■ Late foetuses in countries with poor standards of neonatal care may not be viable as early in the gestation period as the same late foetuses in more developed countries. Clearly, claiming that an entities moral status should depend on where its mother is residing at the time is nonsensical.

- If we could determine the actual day that a foetus became viable, then what specifically has changed, from the day before, to justify its change in moral status?

Similarly, with the birth threshold. The obvious objection here is to compare, say, a twenty-nine-week-old *in utero* foetus with a baby, born prematurely, at twenty-nine weeks gestation. How can being one side of the vaginal canal, or the other, make such a difference to an entity's moral status? This objection is particularly effective in arguing with people who, while defending abortion, have a moral objection to infanticide.

Nevertheless, those claiming that personhood is obtained at conception, have difficult questions to answer themselves!

Consider another thought experiment – *The Embryo Rescue Case*:

> You are in a hospital and suddenly there is a catastrophic fire which will soon destroy it. In the corridor you are walking down there are two rooms, one containing a newborn baby and another containing a canister with five frozen embryos scheduled for implantation in women who cannot conceive naturally. You only have time to save either the baby or the canister. Which one do you choose?

Almost everyone confronted with this scenario opts to rescue the baby. But this common intuition presents a problem for anyone believing that all human beings are morally considerable *persons* from conception. Surely, rescuing the five embryos, instead of the one baby, is the morally right action to take, although this is unacceptable to most people!

Also, if the conception threshold is correct then, as we discovered in the previous chapter, modern embryology informs us that the majority of people who have ever existed perished long before they were born! This makes spontaneous miscarriage the single biggest cause of human fatality, surpassing causes like natural disasters, malnutrition and cancer by a massive margin. The natural implication would be that significantly large amounts of money and medical resources should be diverted to investigating and trying to eliminate this condition.

One of the strongest arguments against *personhood* being acquired at conception is twinning. Consider, for example, Abigail and Brittany Hensel (pictured right). Born in 1990, they are dicephalic parapagus[68]  twins. Although originating from a single zygote, they consider themselves, and are considered to be, two individual *persons*. They both graduated with Bachelor of Arts degrees in 2012, and each had to take their own

---

[68] Dicephalus means two-headed and Parapagus means joined side by side.

driving test. So, the obvious question is: When did their single zygote become two *persons*?

If we are to make any progress here, it would appear that blindly accepting the punctualist view of the acquisition of personhood creates more problems than it solves. So, let's go back a step and examine what, exactly, we mean by the concept of *person*.

The easiest way of looking at the concept of *personhood* and how it relates to the biological definition of a *human being*, is to consider each as a *set* and then decide which entities fit into each set.

We can consider three options:

Figure 1 illustrates the case where being a *human* is both a *necessary* and a *sufficient* condition to be a *person*. Notice that both *sets* completely overlap, *viz.* all *human beings* are *persons* and nothing that is not *human* can be a person.

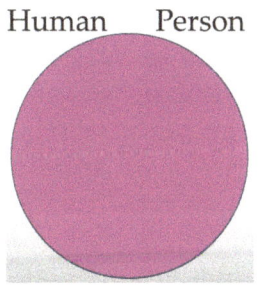

Figure 1

All through history some thinkers have created a seemingly impenetrable barrier between us and other animals. As the French philosopher, mathematician, and scientist Rene Descartes (1596–1650) put it:

"Animals are mere machines, but man stands alone."

However, many philosophers reject this option, considering it to be **speciesism**; the privileging of human species membership over non-human animals whose cognitive abilities may equal and even exceed those of young children and the mentally impaired.

This leads us to Figure 2, where the set of all *humans* becomes a subset of the more inclusive set of *persons*. Notice, that with this option, as with the first, being a *human* is a *sufficient* condition for being a *person* but, in this case, not a *necessary* one. So, what might also be included in the set of *Persons*?

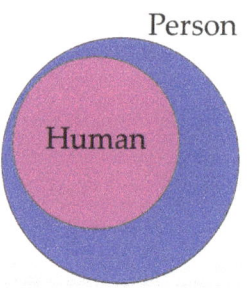

Figure 2

Well, the early Christian philosopher and theologian Boethius (c. 480-525) formulated what became the standard Western definition of a "person," namely "an individual substance of a rational nature." In his work *A Treatise Against Eutyches and Nestorius*, we have the following:

> Now from all the definitions we have given it is clear that **Person** cannot be affirmed of bodies which have no life (for no one ever said that a stone had a person), nor yet of living things which lack sense (for neither is there any person of a tree), **nor finally of that which is bereft of mind and reason** (for there is no person of a horse or ox or any other of the animals which dumb and unreasoning live a life of sense alone), **but we say there is a person of a man, of God, of all angel. ...**

> Wherefore if Person belongs to substances alone, and these rational, and if every nature is a substance, existing not in universals but in individuals, **we have found the definition of Person**, viz.: **"The individual substance of a rational creature."**

So, those people believing in a god (or gods) and angels could include them in the *Person* set along with *human beings*. Those ethicists advocating for animal *rights* might also want to include sentient animals in this set. As Charles Darwin (1809–82) wrote, in the *Descent of Man* "There is no fundamental difference between man and the higher mammals in their mental faculties" and that all the differences are "of degree, not of kind". In addition, individuals hypothesising the existence of intelligent extra-terrestrials, or the possibility of sentient androids, might want to include them too.

However, Figure 3 illustrates another option where, like the second option, being a *human* is not a *necessary* condition for inclusion in the set of *persons*, but neither is it a

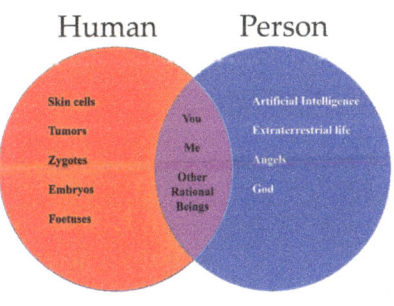

Figure 3

sufficient condition. As zygotes, embryos, foetuses do not possess any of the criteria typically associated with an adult, normally functioning, individual, such as sentience, reasoning ability, agency (i.e. the ability for self-motivated activity), etc., then they are not included in the set of *persons*.

Here we can see a clear distinction between two views on *personhood* – the **Endowment View** and the **Performance (or Functional) View**. The endowment view, which encompasses both options 1 and 2 above, considers each *human being* as having inherent moral worth, simply by virtue of the kind of being it is. The performance view, by contrast, only accords moral respect to beings if, and only if, they function in a given way. In addition, these functions or abilities must be present in *actual*, not just *potential*, form. Various ethicists have put forward suggestions for what functions a *human being* needs in order to be classed as a *person*, e.g. sentience, self-awareness, minimum intelligence and reasoning ability. As a human's ability to *function* as a *person*, gradually increases as they age and develop, this view is more, or less, synonymous with the idea of **gradualism** introduced above.

One way of making progress here is to consider the case of *Baby Theresa*. In Florida, in 1992, an infant known to the public as "Baby Theresa" was born anencephalic. Although such babies are often referred to as "babies without brains," this is not strictly accurate, as the brain stem is present and so autonomic bodily functions, such as breathing, and blood circulation are still possible. Crucially, what is missing are the cerebrum and the cerebellum (as well as the top of the scull). In recent times, cases of anencephaly are usually detected during pregnancy and the foetuses typically aborted.

Those that are not aborted are either stillborn or die within a few days of birth. In Baby Theresa's case, the diagnosis came too late for an abortion or induced labour, and doctors advised that she would need to be carried to full-term.

On hearing the news, and before the birth, her parents Laura Campo and Justin Pearson, hoping that something good could come from their heartache, requested that Baby Theresa's organs be used for immediate transplant, with the agreement of the attending physicians.

However, despite Baby Theresa not having either consciousness, or even the possibility of consciousness, the hospital refused their request to declare Baby Theresa dead, so that her tiny organs could be harvested and donated to other needy children. It turns out that Floridian law did not allow a person to be declared dead while any part of their brain was functioning. By the time Baby Theresa eventually died, nine days after birth, her organs had decayed to the point where they could not be used.

Clearly, Baby Theresa was a *human being*, but should she have been included in the set of *persons*? Well, imagine that you had the onerous task of adjudicating on the ethics of this case. Ignoring the Floridian legal system, how could you proceed?

The dilemma faced in such cases as this has been characterized as an issue of Kantian versus utilitarian ethics, so it will help to have a basic understanding of both.

Immanuel Kant (1724–1804) was a German philosopher most famous for his *Categorical Imperative*, which he expresses in three forms, the most widely known of which is formally called the *Formula of Universal Law*:

> Act only according to that maxim by which you can at the same time will that it should become a universal law. *Foundations of the Metaphysics of Morals.*

Kant believed that human beings occupy a special place in creation, separated from the rest of the animal kingdom by their faculty of **practical reason**, *viz.* the capacity of rational beings to act in accordance with principles that they give themselves. For him ethics and freedom were intimately connected; human beings could not be free if they simply followed whatever the laws of nature urged them to do. However, *rationality* gives them something that no other animal seems to have, i.e. the ability to overcome the laws of nature by giving themselves laws to follow. He called the action of giving laws to oneself *autonomy*.

For example, nature (probably for good evolutionary reasons) draws you to devour sweet foods. However, you know that consuming too much of them is not good for you, and so you can decide for yourself to limit your intake of such foods. By adopting this *law*, you are doing a lot more than avoiding unnecessary calories; you are acting independently of the law of nature and have now become *free*.

Another form of the categorical imperative, which is particularly relevant to our case is formally called the *Formula of Humanity*:

> "Act in such a way that you treat humanity, whether in your own **person** or in the **person** of any other, never merely as a means to an end, but always at the same time as an end." *Grounding for the Metaphysics of Morals*

Put very simply, Kantian ethics prohibits using one person (even yourself) merely for the sake of another.

Utilitarianism, in contrast, is a form of consequentialism. Although proto-utilitarian views can be detected throughout the history of ethical theory, the first systematic account was developed by the English philosopher Jeremy Bentham (1748–1832). It can be best summed up by his quote:

> The greatest happiness of the greatest number is the foundation of **morals** and **legislation**.

So, one practical way of tackling the question of whether Baby Theresa was a *person*, and whether we should use her organs for transplants, would be to reduce the problem to logical arguments. Using Kantian ethics, you could argue thus:

KP1. It is always wrong to use people merely as means to other people's ends.

KP2. Baby Theresa is a person.

KP3. Taking Baby Theresa's organs would be using her merely as a means to benefit other children.

Therefore

C. It would be wrong to take Baby Theresa's organs.

However, a utilitarian argument could be:

UP1. If we can benefit other people without causing harm to anyone else, we *ought* to do it.

UP2. Transplanting the organs would benefit other children without harming Baby Theresa.

Therefore

C. We *ought* to transplant the organs.

Notice that both arguments are **valid,** and so we know that, if the premises are true, then the conclusions are also true. However, these arguments have conflicting conclusions! This means that, at least one argument must have at least one false premise. So, the question is: which premise, or premises, is/are false?

Instinctively, people disagreeing with the utilitarian position could argue that killing Baby Theresa would be causing her harm, but is that really the case? She cannot *experience* pain; in fact, she cannot *experience* anything at all! She is not conscious, nor can she ever be conscious, and within a few days she will be dead.

However, her organs have the potential not only to benefit several actual recipients but their families as well. In addition, Laura Campo and Justin Pearson will derive some comfort from knowing that something good has come out of their tragedy and that their baby's life has had some positive outcome. The utilitarian argument in favour of transplantation, in this case, therefore, seems compelling.

But what about the first premise in the Kantian argument, that it is always wrong to use people merely as means to other people's ends? Using people, in the Kantian sense, normally involves infringing on their *autonomy* – their ability to decide for themselves how to live their own lives. However, Baby Theresa is not *autonomous* and never will be. She has no desires or values and cannot decide for herself how to live her life. The proscription against using people would appear, therefore, not to apply in this case.

Notice that the Kantian argument assumes that Baby Theresa is a *person*. However, for Kant, as we have seen above, what separates human beings from the rest of the animal kingdom and, therefore, gives them moral value, is their capacity for practical reason and their ability to act *autonomously*, neither of which Baby Theresa has. Kant himself would not, therefore, have considered Baby Theresa to be a *person*!

This final point is important because some anti-abortionists have tried to use Kant's *Formula of Humanity* by arguing that it applies to all members of the species *Homo Sapiens*; zygotes, embryos and foetuses included. However, this claim is easily refuted by examining Kant's philosophy.

For Kant, everything that exists has two natures:

- the **phenomenon** (or empirical) part, which can be known through the senses and which is subject to physical causal laws.
- the **noumenal** (i.e. non-empirical) part, which is the essence of a thing; the *thing-in-itself*.

When it comes to humans, the phenomenon part is simply the physical, instinctual, self, which for Kant was specifically excluded from his ethical theory. Consider, for example, if a dog bites you, it is acting on instinct and cannot be held morally responsible for its actions.

The noumenal part, on the other hand, is the purely intelligible, rational, self which exists independently of causal laws. Not being governed by causal laws, it is free to choose how to behave. And, as we have already noted, it is this freedom to act autonomously that, for Kant, gives humans their moral worth.

Crucially, our moral agency cannot be connected in any way with our biological nature. Mark Sagoff, who before retiring was a Professor of Philosophy at George Mason University, Fairfax, Virginia, makes the following point, when referring to extracorporeal human embryos (EHE's):

> It is impossible to attribute moral status to an EHE on grounds of its **physical characteristics** alone – **even when its potential is considered** – because there is no point in the process of ontogeny at which a scientific finding can

be made, as it were, that a glob of protoplasm is now sufficiently endowed with moral freedom that it has become a responsible agent or sufficiently endowed with cultural, aesthetic, and ethical capacities that it has become a human being. *Extracorporeal Embryos and Three Conception of the Human.*

For Kant, moral value supervenes on our biological selves only when we develop the capacity for rational thought:

> Beings whose existence depends not on our will but on nature's, have nevertheless, if they are irrational beings, only a relative value as means, and are therefore called things; **rational beings, on the contrary, are called persons**, because their very nature points them out as ends in themselves, that is as some-thing which must not be used merely as means, and so far therefore restricts freedom of action (and is an object of respect). *The Metaphysics of Morals.*

Anti-abortionists, trying to employ Kant's *Formula of Humanity*, however, seem to forget that there is an actual *person* involved in the pregnancy, i.e. the pregnant woman who is seeking an abortion.

I am quite sure that, for any woman wanting a child, the inconvenience, discomfort, pain and risks of pregnancy and childbirth are a *price worth paying*. But what about a woman who does not want a child, at least at this time? Clearly, trying to force her to have the baby would be a serious violation of Kant's *Formula of Humanity*, a key aspect of which is to respect the ends rational agents have chosen for themselves. It would not only be ignoring her rational and autonomous decision, but actively attempting to thwart it!

At first glance, the moral legitimacy of abortion seems to stand or fall on how we answer the question "Is a foetus a *person* with the same moral status as you or me?" However, the question itself appears to be philosophically intractable. This is because, as the American philosopher and jurist Ronald Dworkin (1931–2013) expressed it, in his book *Life's Dominion: An Argument about Abortion, Euthanasia, and Individual Freedom*:

> One side thinks that a human fetus is already a moral subject, an unborn child, from the moment of conception. The other thinks that a just-conceived fetus is merely a collection of cells under the command not of a brain but of only a genetic code, no more a child, yet, than a just-fertilized egg is a chicken. Neither side can offer any argument that the other must accept - there is no biological fact waiting to be discovered or crushing moral analogy waiting to be invented that can dispose of the matter.

In other words, there are no irrefutably convincing facts or arguments that would compel one side of the argument to concede victory to the other. Nevertheless, with one side calling for abortions to be made illegal, whilst the other side is calling for current legal restrictions to be lifted, we cannot just leave the question of the morality of abortion up in the air. So, how do we make progress?

It would seem that both ethicists and legislators are asking too much of the term *personhood*. Everyone can agree that a normally functioning, sentient and rational human being is a *person* and that at some time during that entity's development *personhood* has been acquired. Taking account of the Hensel twins, and in fact all monozygotic twins, it would appear that the claim that *personhood* is acquired at conception is singularly unconvincing.

Adopting the *performance view* of *personhood* acquisition, however, allows parents and society to grant increasing moral status and, therefore, responsibility as a child ages and matures. We wouldn't for example let a physically capable twelve-year-old drive a car on the public highway.

The two main arguments against accepting this view are that it is arbitrary and does not rule out infanticide.

We can dismiss the arbitrary argument simply on the grounds that society sets arbitrary milestones purely for practical reasons. It needs, for example, to rule on when a child must start and end compulsory education, at what age someone can work, operate dangerous machinery, get a driving licence, vote, and marry.

The infanticide argument, however, needs to be taken very seriously.

Infanticide was, up until comparatively recently, one of the most commonly practiced social norms in human history, with virtually every civilization adopting it. It was, for example, a safer means of population control than abortion. Sex selective infanticide (in reality female infanticide) was widespread, usually for financial reasons. The influential Greek philosopher Aristotle, who we encountered in Chapter 4, declared that no deformed child should live, and in the Middle Ages an infant born with physical defects or behavioural abnormalities would often be considered an evil omen or the product of demonic supernatural forces. Such children would often be killed by their parents or community, who deemed the child a threat. So, for the vast majority of human history, the killing of newborn infants was considered totally acceptable and, when practiced to ward off evil forces or reduce the expansion of a growing population, morally virtuous.

Today, we no longer believe that children born with physical or mental abnormalities are the result of an evil supernatural force or consider them to be a bad omen. Instead, all newborn babies are considered vulnerable and deserving of protection. Unwanted children can be put up for adoption or handed over to the state.

So, as attitudes to children have changed depending on the cultural environment they were born into, not to mention our changing attitudes towards sentient animals, or possible extra-terrestrials, arguing about what exactly *personhood* signifies, or when it is acquired, is likely to prove fruitless!

There is, however, another approach which may prove beneficial, and that is by making a distinction between **moral agents** and **moral patients**.

A moral agent can be defined as someone who can understand moral reasons and who can choose to act for those reasons. Additionally, we can hold these people morally responsible for their actions. A moral patient, on the other hand, can be defined as something that cannot be expected to act for moral reasons, but to which moral agents can be said to have some responsibility towards. With these definitions in mind, foetuses, young children, sentient animals and even the environment, can be considered as possible candidates as moral patients.

Notice that the concept of a moral agent corresponds nicely with Kant's idea of "rational beings" who, crucially, should be treated as "ends in themselves." In other words, moral agents should treat each other equally and with the same respect they would expect other people to treat them, regardless of religious or gender differences!

The fact that babies and young children, existing as separate individuals, are included under the *umbrella* of moral patients would be enough to give them the moral and legal protection against infanticide.

Having dealt at some length, with the morality of abortion, the next chapter will consider the legal implications of everything we have examined so far.

Chapter 6

Abortion and the Law

No woman wants an abortion as she wants an ice cream cone or a Porsche. She wants an abortion as an animal caught in a trap wants to gnaw off its own leg. *Frederica Mathewes-Green (1952-) American author.*

At the heart of liberty is the right to define one's own concept of existence, of meaning, of the universe, and of the mystery of human life. *Justice Anthony Kennedy (1936 -) American lawyer and jurist.*

In the previous chapter, I considered the morality of abortion and highlighted the intractability of the ethical arguments over the concept of *personhood*. I pointed out that this had particular relevance in the US owing to the fact that if the unborn[69], at any stage in their development, were classed as *persons*, then their *right to life* would be protected under the Constitution.

In this chapter, I want to demonstrate that, although people have very different opinions about the *personhood* of the unborn, and hence the morality of abortion, any legislation restricting it should not be influenced by anti-abortion rhetoric but should be confined to questions concerning the *right to life* that

---

[69] I will use the term **unborn** simply as an umbrella term to include zygotes, blastocysts, embryos and foetuses.

the unborn *might* make claim to, when confronted with a pregnant woman's *right* to bodily autonomy.

We can begin by noting that some things can be considered immoral whilst there is no law against them, nor should there be! Adultery and lying to a friend are just two examples of actions most people consider as immoral, but which are not against the law, at least currently in the UK! The following legal case should highlight the point I am making. Although it involves the American legal system, I believe it has both moral and legal relevance for us in the UK. The case is McFall v. Shimp.

In July 1978, a thirty-nine-year-old unmarried asbestos worker, Robert McFall, was suffering "from a rare bone marrow disease" called aplastic anaemia. Without an urgent bone marrow transfusion, McFall would soon die. McFall's first cousin, a 42-year-old crane worker named David Shimp, was the only available bone marrow match for McFall at the time, but Shimp refused to donate his bone marrow, which would have dramatically increased the odds of saving McFall's life. McFall then sued Shimp in order to force him to donate his bone marrow. When the case ended up in court, although the judge commented that Shimp's position was "**morally** indefensible," he could not force Shimp to donate his bone marrow. Judge Flaherty also stated that forcing a person to submit to an intrusion of his body in order to donate bone marrow "would defeat the **sanctity of the individual** and would impose a rule which would know no limits, and one could not imagine where the line would be drawn."

Clearly, there is no doubt that McFall was a *person*, with the same full moral status as you and I. However most, if not all, people would agree that, whilst donating bone marrow to save the life of another *human being*, whether related to them or not, would be a morally virtuous thing to do – an act of *Good Samaritanism* if you like – the law should not be able to compel you to do so. In other words, being a *person*, with a *right to life*, does not give anyone the *right* to use another person's bone marrow, even if they need that person's bone marrow to go on living. And, as there is nothing special about bone marrow, we can generalize the above conclusion as follows:

> Being a *person* and having the *right to life*, does not give you the right to use another person's body, even if you need that person's body to go on living.

This case highlights a limitation on the *right to life*, that is not usually recognized, especially among anti-abortionists, namely, that the *right to life* does not include, or entail, the right to be provided with the use, or the continued use, of whatever is needed in order for you to go on living!

The relevance for the legality of abortion is obvious, the unborn do not have the *right* to use a woman's body against her will, even if they need that woman's body to go on living!

One argument sometimes employed by anti-abortionist is that pregnancy is a *sui generis* situation, viz. constituting a class of its own. Therefore, any attempt to use other situations as analogous to pregnancy are bound to fail. In the above case, for example, they try to argue that Shimp did nothing to cause McFall to be dependent on him. The clear implication being that any woman who has sex is responsible for any unintended pregnancy and now has a responsibility to bring the resulting foetus to term. What these anti-abortionists fail to acknowledge, or choose not to, is that any thought experiment, or reference to previous legal cases, are purely intended to bring out a *principle* which is either universally, or at least generally, accepted within society at large. If you accept, as most people do, that being a *person* and having a *right to life*, does not give you the right to use another person's body, even if you need that person's body to go on living, then the McFall v. Shimp case has served its purpose.

It is also important to keep in mind that any law restricting or banning abortion will apply to all citizens of the state and not just the ones that, for example, have unprotected sex with multiple partners.

Consider, for a moment, a young humanist couple – Mary and Joseph – who are very much in love. They both work hard and have good jobs. They have saved up enough money for a deposit on a house, which they have now purchased with the help of a substantial mortgage. They are married and have decided that, although they want children, they cannot bring a child into "an environment conducive to the realization of his or her full potential[70]" at this time. However, they do

---

[70] To quote from the United Methodist Church's *Resolution on Responsible Parenthood*.

enjoy having sex (with each other) and so, being a responsible couple, they use some method of birth control. Unfortunately, no method of birth control (except total abstinence) is 100% reliable, and Mary finds herself pregnant. After talking it over with each other, both Mary and Joseph agree that she should have an abortion.

Just to be clear, the illustration below depicts a 3–4-week-old embryo, an entity roughly 0.014 of an inch in size. Now, anti-abortionists claim that Mary's embryo is alive and human, which it unarguably is. In addition, they claim that this innocent *child* was put in its current situation because Mary chose to have sex and is therefore now responsible for it. If Mary intends to have an abortion, then laws should be put in place which, in effect, try to force her to carry it to term.

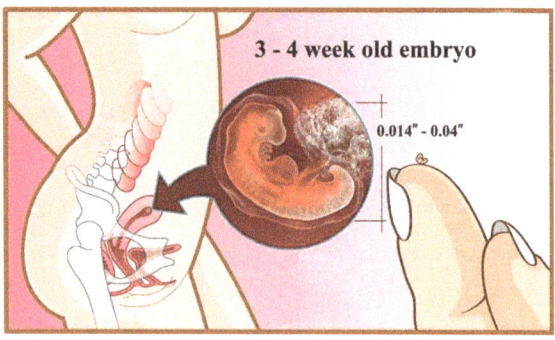

I am quite sure that Mary would accept the fact that the embryo growing inside her is undeniably *human*. However, it certainly isn't conscious or self-aware; it cannot perceive pain (or anything else for that matter) and will not suffer any regret about not being born! She considers it as nothing more than "a collection of cells under the command not of a brain but of only a genetic code, no more a child, yet, than a just-fertilized egg is a chicken," to quote from Ronald Dworkin. Any law preventing her from having an abortion would, therefore, be depriving her of her *right* to bodily autonomy.

I should state, at this stage, that if gestation was a completely benign activity that did not result in any inconvenience at all to the pregnant women, then the anti-abortionist case would be morally stronger; although, as can be inferred from the McFall v. Shimp case, not necessarily legally so.

However, the physical and psychological risks of bringing an unwanted pregnancy to term can be significant and even life threatening. Just consider nausea and vomiting for example. According to the National Health Service (NHS), around 8 out of every 10 pregnant women feel sick, are sick, or both during pregnancy. Although, most of the time, these symptoms are mild, around 1 to 3 in every 100 pregnant women suffer from hyperemesis gravidarum (extreme and persistent nausea and vomiting during pregnancy), often requiring hospital treatment.

Other complications during pregnancy include anaemia, gestational hypertension, gestational diabetes, mild to severe pre-eclampsia, and pregnancy related depression and anxiety, to mention just a few.

Aside from the medical complications that just being pregnant can bring, there is also the pain, and possible medical complications, of labour and delivery to consider. For example, the NHS states that 9 in every 10 first time mothers, who have a vaginal birth, will experience a tear, graze, or episiotomy[71]. Perineal[72] tears, whilst common, are usually minor and heal quickly. However, 6% of first-time mothers suffer from an obstetric anal sphincter injury (OASI), requiring a trip to the operating theatre for stitching. I don't think I need mention the possible risks involved with a caesarean section.

It is somewhat telling that, according to the World Health Organization, the **maternal mortality ratio**[73] (MMR) is considered one of the main indicators of a country's status in the area of maternal health. Although this figure has gone down, in the United Kingdom, in recent years, the figure for 2017 was 7.0. That is 7 deaths for every 100,000 live births! According to the Centers for Disease Control and Prevention (CDC)[74], the figure was higher in the United States in 2018, at 17.4! In comparison, the Office for National Statistics have a spreadsheet showing that no deaths occurred between 2015 to 2019 for medical abortions (i.e. taking medicine to end the pregnancy). The CDC also have a

---

[71] An episiotomy is a surgical incision of the perineum to enlarge the vagina to aid delivery.

[72] The perineum is the area between a woman's vaginal opening and anus.

[73] The annual number of women who die during pregnancy and childbirth per 100,000 live births.

[74] https://www.cdc.gov/nchs/pressroom/nchs_press_releases/2020/202001_MMR.htm

severe maternal morbidity (SMM) measure[75] which "has been steadily increasing in recent years and affected more than 50,000 women in the United States in 2014."

Taking the above into consideration, it is not surprising that the UN Special Rapporteur on Torture[76] has called for the decriminalizing of abortion and for states to ensure "access to legal and safe abortions, at a minimum in cases of rape, incest and severe or fatal fetal impairment and where the life or physical or mental health of the mother is at risk."

As I stated, in the previous chapter, for any woman wanting a child, these symptoms and risks are usually considered a *price worth paying*, but one question we need to answer is: should a legal system try to compel women who do not want a child at this time to face them?

Returning to Mary's decision to have an abortion. As a responsible adult, Mary was using what was considered to be one of the most effective methods of contraception, because she definitely did not wish to become pregnant at this time!

However, according to a report[77] on the British Pregnancy Advisory Service (BPAS) website, 24.2% of

---

[75] Although there is no agreed definition for SMM, it "can be thought of as unintended outcomes of the process of labor and delivery that result in significant short-term or long-term consequences to a woman's health."

[76] See United Nations A/HRC/31/57.

[77] www.bpas.org/about-our-charity/press-office/press-releases/women-cannot-control-fertility-through-contraception-alone-bpas-

women who had an abortion at BPAS clinics in 2016 were using the "most effective methods of contraception." The report goes on to state:

> No method of contraception is 100% effective, yet public discourse and some family planning initiatives frequently imply that abortion can always be avoided through the use of contraception. However, each year **9 in every 100** women using the contraceptive pill, the most popular method of contraception in the UK, **6 in every 100** using the contraceptive injection, and nearly **1 in every 100** using the IUD (copper coil), will become pregnant.

In that same report, Ann Furedi their Chief Executive states:

> **"The answer to unsafe abortion is not contraception, it is safe abortion.** When you encourage women to use contraception, you give them the sense that they can control their fertility – but if you do not provide safe abortion services when that contraception fails you are doing them a great disservice. **Our data shows women cannot control their fertility through contraception alone, even when they are using some of the most effective methods.** Family planning is contraception and abortion. **Abortion is birth control that women need when their regular method lets them down."**

Now, imagine that you are appointed to a committee tasked with reviewing the current abortion law and

---

data-shows-1-in-4-woman-having-an-abortion-were-using-most-effective-contraception making recommendations where changes were thought necessary. One way of proceeding would be to see if any relevant *principles* could be employed from previous case law. As we saw above, the case of McFall v. Shimp clearly illustrates that, even if the unborn have a *right to life*, that *right to life* does not include, or entail, the right to be provided with the use, or the continued use, of whatever is needed in order for the unborn to go on living, especially when consideration is given to the physical and mental health of the woman involved.

It is important to consider, at this stage, the fact that the debate on abortion in England and most of Europe, as well as in America, is occurring in pluralist, mainly secular, societies. Consequently, not only does the debate involve discussions within particular communities of faith, sharing moral and metaphysical convictions, but it also takes place in the public arena, where common ethical and metaphysical concepts cannot be presupposed. Therefore, much that one might hold as true within one's own community of faith, cannot either be presumed to hold as part of the general moral fabric of a pluralist society, or be forced on it. Therefore, those wishing to participate meaningfully in the debate will need to be able to justify any claims they make on terms agreeable to people holding differing metaphysical and ethical views.

I think most people will accept that, however unlikely, it is not beyond the bounds of possibility that we will one day be visited by an alien race that has been observing us from afar. If they are intelligent, self-aware, friendly, and with a desire for inter-species dialogue and cooperation, it would be difficult to deny them *personhood* status. Yet, these aliens would not be *human beings*! The point is that *human being* and *person* are not conceptually the same thing. It is possible to be a *person* without being a *human being*.

The important question for us, however, is:

Is it possible to be a *human being* without being a *person*?

Some anti-abortionists claim that, even if the terms *human being* and *person* do not mean the same thing, all human beings, by virtue of their *human* biology, are also *persons*, no matter what their current stage of development. However, simply stating that claim, sometimes over and over again, as some anti-abortionists are prone to do, does not make it true! What they fail to acknowledge, or even recognize, is the crucial fact that, because the two terms describe conceptually different categories, the need to make an argument connecting the two cannot be circumvented or just simply ignored. Not only that, but anti-abortionists would need to argue that, unlike any other *person* (including you and me), the unborn have a moral right to instrumentalize another *person* (the pregnant woman) for sustenance even against her wishes!

Although, as we saw in the previous chapter, defining the term *personhood* in a way that achieves universal agreement has not yet been achieved, I think it is fair to say that most people would recognize a *person* when they see one, and a single celled zygote, barely visible to the naked eye, would not be included.

Recognizing that just claiming that a zygote, being *human*, automatically endows it with actual *personhood*, is singularly unconvincing, some anti-abortionists have tried claiming that, because gestation is a continuous, unbroken, process of development, and that the zygote will eventually become an individual with full *personhood*, it should be classed as a *potential* person with the same *right to life*, that any *actual* person would have.

However, there are at least three arguments against this view:

1. Something with the *potential* to become an X is, by definition, not an *actual* X. Once something becomes an *actual* X, it clearly loses its *potential* to become an X.
2. By way of analogy, an acorn, through a continuous, unbroken, process of development, has the *potential* to become an oak tree. However, you would not call an acorn an oak tree.
3. Imagine that you are unfortunate enough to require an operation for some medical problem. You attend the hospital only to be informed, by an administrator, that the person scheduled to operate on you is a first-year medical student. The administrator then attempts to reassure you by saying that the medical student has the *potential* to become an *actual* surgeon once he has completed all his training!

Some anti-abortionists try referring to Scripture, claiming that, as "man is made in the image of God," a human being has moral status and a *right to life* from the moment of conception.

First, we need to bear in mind that this claim is based on Genesis 1:27 a verse in the Old Testament; that is Hebrew scripture. As I covered, in Chapter 2, traditional Jews regarded the embryo "to be mere water until the 40th day." And today, regardless of any advance in their knowledge of embryology (or probably because of it), the State of Israel has one of the most relaxed attitudes to abortion you will find anywhere in the world.

Secondly, it needs to be acknowledged that there is a basic difference between religious and secular ethics, in that, whilst the various religions regard moral choices as an expression of the fundamental *beliefs* and values that its followers hold, secular ethics justifies moral choices through rational argument and reflection. That being the case, a secularist could legitimately question a Christian about how their various *beliefs* might apply to abortion. Based on what we have covered in the book so far, I can see the question-and-answer session going something like the following:

Secularist: Do you believe that God is omniscient and, if so, what do you understand the term to mean?

Christian[78]: Yes, I do. An equivalent term would be *all-knowing*, *viz.* God has perfect

---

[78] Because of the estimated 41,000 Christian denominations and organizations currently across the world, this conversation can only

knowledge of events that have already happened, are currently happening, and will happen in the future. Along with perfect knowledge, he also has perfect understanding and perfect wisdom as to how to apply that knowledge.

Secularist: Do you believe that God creates individual immortal souls at the appropriate time, either at conception or at some later time before birth.

Christian: Yes, each soul is created by God and infused at the moment of conception, which we consider to be as soon as the sperm and the ovum unite to form a zygote.

Secularist: Do you believe that God is omnipotent and, if so, what do understand the term to mean?

Christian: Yes, I do. An equivalent term would be *all-powerful*, meaning that God has the power to do anything that it is logically possible to do. He could not, for example, make a square circle, but that does not imply any real limitations on his power.

Secularist: Ok then. So, if God is omniscient, then he will know if a pregnant woman

be representative of commonly held *beliefs* within the main denominations.

intends to have an abortion. If she does, then he needn't create a soul for that particular zygote. Failing that, as souls are immortal, the act of abortion will not kill it, and God can simply infuse it into another zygote, if he should so choose. Also, being omnipotent, he could actually stop the pregnant woman from having an abortion in the first place. Not only that, but he is supposed to have issued commands for humankind to obey, such as 'you shall not murder' and, 'you shall not steal.' So, if he did want to prohibit abortion, he could simply have issued one other command such as, 'you shall not procure an abortion!' After all, Jews reckon that there are 613 commandments in the Torah, some as seemingly trivial as, 'You shall not cook a goat in its mother's milk' (Ex 34:26) and, 'you shall not wear clothes made of wool and linen woven together' (Deut. 22:11) As abortions are currently performed, and have been for centuries, it would seem that they cannot be against God's will!

Christian: Hmm! I'll get back to you.

This final Christian comment is one I receive from Jehovah's Witnesses, and other fundamentalist Christians, who knock at my door and who believe the Bible is inerrant, when I point out some glaringly obvious contradictions in it! I am sure that some

Christians will claim that this is not how a *proper* debate on abortion should go, but it would be interesting to hear any specific refutation.

It should be noted here that, although the upper echelon of the Catholic Church continues to declare[79] that "From the first moment of his existence, a human being must be recognized as having the rights of a person", this statement does not meet the definition of an **infallible teaching**[80] for Catholics. I pointed out, in Chapter 4, that the document *Declaration on Procured Abortion* contains, in its *Notes*, the admission that "This declaration expressly leaves aside the question of the moment when the spiritual soul is infused. There is not a unanimous tradition on this point and authors are as yet in disagreement." Furthermore, a survey, carried out by the Pew Research Center in 2019, showed that 56% of Catholics in the US said that abortion should be legal in all/most cases, while 21% said it should be legal in **all** cases.

Also, in Chapter 4, I quoted the Catholic apologist Trent Horn, from his book *Persuasive Pro-life*, where he states that:

> There is simply no way the state can be neutral on the question of when **life begins**, because if there can be any laws at all that protect **human beings**, the state has

---

[79] Catechism 2270.
[80] The Catholic Church teaches that infallibility is a charism (spiritual gift) entrusted by Christ to the whole church, whereby the Pope enjoys papal infallibility.

to make a decision on who counts as a **human being** and who doesn't under those laws. Pro-life advocates simply maintain that the state should endorse an answer to the question of when **life begins,** or who counts as a **human being** with a **right to life,** that is backed **by science** and **common sense.**

So, let's have a look at what two distinguished scientists and science writers, Harold J. Morowitz and James S. Trefil, investigating what modern biology can contribute to our understanding of the abortion debate, had to say in their excellent book *The Facts of Life: Science and the Abortion Controversy.* In the *Summary* they state:

> Whether we start by looking at other forms of life that exist today or trace the development of our species through time, **we see that what distinguishes human beings from other forms of life, both structurally and functionally, is the existence of a large, multiply connected cerebral cortex.** In our usage, we say that our species acquired humanness when the enlarged cortex developed, **and the individual human fetus acquires humanness when the cortex begins to function.** *P.152.*

Here they are using the term *humanness* to mean "those properties that distinguish human beings from other living things." In Chapter 5, they had already written that:

> Identifying **humanness** with the cerebral cortex and its functions is not a particularly revolutionary (or even particularly original) proposition. Scientists **and theologians** have long put this view forward. Teilhard

de Chardin, a Jesuit scholar, argued that humankind's transcendence hinged on the development of the cerebral cortex. Another Catholic theologian, Bernard Häring, argued in the 1970's that **the cerebral cortex is the center of all personal manifestations and activities,** and anatomist Paul Glees wrote in 1988 that **"the [cerebral cortex] represents the signature of a genetically unique person."**

The functions of the cerebral cortex include, for example, rational thinking, planning, speech production, perception of oneself and the social environment. In other words, functions that we associate with a normal *person*. Morowitz and Trefil put the time that a foetus possesses a fully functioning cerebral cortex at no earlier than the twenty-fourth week which, coincidently, is the point at which a foetus is currently considered to be viable outside the mother's body.

In the first seven chapters of their book the authors tried to be as objective and impartial as possible. However, in the *Afterword* they gave their personal views and James Trefil has this to say:

> In an ideal world, in fact, there would be no abortion debate. Every child would be wanted; every fetus would be surrounded by a constellation of adults waiting joyously to nourish it and bring it to a happy adulthood. There would be no conflict of rights, because every pregnant woman would have chosen to use her body to produce a child.
>
> But we don't live in an ideal world. Conception can (and does) occur as a result of rape and incest. It occurs because people are careless, and it occurs because, even

when they're careful, no method of birth control is perfect. It does no good to tell someone, "You should have been more careful," even if it's true, because you are still faced with the question of what to do about the pregnancy.

In the end the abortion controversy comes down to one question: Will *this* particular pregnancy be terminated or not? There are only two possible choices, neither good. One is to abort the fetus. The other is to demand that the pregnancy be brought to term and, in effect, to compel the birth of an unwanted child.

The second choice is repugnant to me. Not only does it entail **real and immediate risks for the mother**, but it may create **a lifetime of misery for the child** – misery that will, in all likelihood, persist for generations. Frankly, **I can imagine fewer human acts more deeply evil than bringing an unwanted child into the world**.

Next, consider a legal case closer to home. The conjoined twins known to the British public as Mary and Jodie, the children of a Maltese couple Michaelangelo and Rina Attard.

When Rina discovered that she was pregnant with conjoined twins, she realized that the health-care facilities on Gozo, where the couple were living, could not handle such a birth. So, the couple came to St Mary's Hospital in Manchester. The twins were born on 8 August 2000, joined at the lower abdomen, with their spines fused and with one properly functioning heart and one properly functioning pair of lungs between them. The doctors said that, without separating Mary and Jodie, they would both die within six months. However, although separating them would save Jodie,

Mary, whose heart and lungs were not properly formed, would die immediately. Their parents, devout Catholics, refused to give permission for the operation, claiming that it would hasten Mary's death. The hospital, hoping to save Jodie, petitioned the courts for permission to carry out the operation anyway.

Commenting on the case, the then Archbishop of Westminster, Cormac Murphy-O'Connor (1932–2017), said:

> There is a **fundamental moral principle** at stake – no one may commit a wrong action that good may come of it. The parents in this case have made it clear that they love both their children equally and cannot consent to one of them being killed to help the other. I believe this moral instinct is right. It would set a very dangerous precedent to enshrine in English case law that it was ever right to kill a person that good may come of it.

The High Court, however, agreed with the hospital and so the parents appealed. In the Appellate Court all their appeals were dismissed, and the operation was carried out. As expected, Jodie lived, and Mary died.

What is interesting for our examination are the following summary conclusions:

> (v) Every human being's right to life carries with it, **as an intrinsic part of it, rights of bodily integrity and autonomy** - the right to have one's own body whole and intact and (on reaching an age of understanding) **to take decisions about one's own body.**

(vii) In this case the purpose of the operation would be to separate the twins and so give Jodie a reasonably good prospect of a long and reasonably normal life. Mary's death would not be the purpose of the operation, although it would be its inevitable consequence. The operation would give her, even in death, bodily integrity as a human being. **She would die, not because she was intentionally killed, but because her own body cannot sustain her life**.

First, notice how similar conclusion (v) is to the quote by Justice Anthony Kennedy under the chapter heading. This famous quote is taken from an 'Opinion of the Court' in a 1992 Supreme Court case, Planned Parenthood v. Casey, and it is worth examining the quote in context:

Our law affords **constitutional protection** to personal decisions relating to marriage, **procreation**, contraception, family relationships, child rearing, and education. ... Our cases recognize "the right of the *individual,* married or single, to be free from unwarranted governmental intrusion into matters so fundamentally affecting a person as the decision whether to bear or beget a child." ... Our precedents "have respected the private realm of family life which the state cannot enter." ... These matters, involving the most intimate and personal choices a person may make in a lifetime, **choices central to personal dignity and autonomy,** are central to the liberty protected by the Fourteenth Amendment. At the heart of liberty is the right to define one's own concept of existence, of meaning, of the universe, and of the mystery of human life. Beliefs about these matters could not define the attributes of personhood were they formed under compulsion of the State.

We can see that both legal systems, in Great Britain and the United States, go to great lengths to protect a *person* from interference with their personal liberty and autonomy. Clearly, trying to force a pregnant woman to carry a baby to term against her wishes would be a serious violation of this principle. It would not only be ignoring her rational and autonomous decision, but actively attempting to thwart it! Such an infringement of her *rights* would be a very grave matter indeed, requiring a compelling argument in order to justify. The onus is, therefore, on the anti-abortionists to come up with such a persuasive argument for their case, rather than the other way around.

Regarding conclusion (vii) and referring back to the McFall v. Shimp case, some anti-abortionists claim that Shimp, by refusing to donate his bone marrow, was not actually killing McFall, just allowing him to die, whereas abortion is the actual killing of a human being. However, the publication *Abortion Statistics, England and Wales: 2019*, shows that medical abortions accounted for 73% of total abortions that year. Medical abortions are carried out using two drugs. The first one to be administered is mifepristone, which blocks the body from producing progesterone, a hormone that the pregnancy needs to carry on growing[81]. So, a medical abortion does not actually kill the foetus, it merely withholds from the foetus what it requires to go on developing and, because it is not viable, it cannot survive outside of the womb once the second drug misoprostol

---

[81] The other drug, misoprostol, causes cramping and bleeding emptying the uterus.

is administered. If this seems like *hair splitting*, then consider the following thought experiment:

> You are living in a state where the law considers that, right from the moment of conception, a human being has all the rights that you and I have. However, we now live at a time when medical science has evolved to the point where it has produced an artificial womb, that can be connect to a suitable adult, male or female, in which a foetus at any stage of development can be transplanted into and brought to term. Now, there is a healthy, normal, two-week old foetus in the womb of a woman who is rapidly dying of some condition that would not affect the foetus until she dies in a few days' time. The state has identified you as the only suitable candidate for an artificial womb to be attached to and the foetus to be transferred into.

Whilst this state may consider it your civic duty, and it may be morally virtuous of you to agree, I don't think many readers would agree to it being legally compelling. Notice, that in this case, you are not killing the foetus, just denying it the means to go on living.

As the artificial womb in the above thought experiment can accept a foetus at any stage of its development, including when it has developed beyond the point where a medical abortion can be performed, the *principle* that the state should not be able to compel you to carry any foetus to term, holds for a pregnant woman needing a surgical abortion.

When considering the effects of any law regarding abortion, it is worth bearing in mind how the law will work in practice and any unintended consequences it might have. We can begin by examining the law as it currently stands in this country and compare it to the American system.

Since the Offences Against the Person Act of 1861, abortion has been a criminal offence in Great Britain and Ireland. However, the Abortion Act 1967 (as amended) allows pregnancies to be terminated, in England, Wales and Scotland, providing certain conditions have been met.

Without going into too much detail, it is sufficient for our purposes to note that, according to the publication *Abortion Statistics, England and Wales: 2019*, 98% of abortions in England and Wales were carried out under Ground C of the Act (section 1(1)(a)):

> That the pregnancy has NOT exceeded its 24th week and that the continuance of the pregnancy would involve risk, greater than if the pregnancy were terminated, of injury to the physical or mental health of the pregnant woman.

The 24th week time limit mentioned here was originally 28 weeks but was reduced in the *Human Fertilisation and Embryology Act 1990*. It refers to the time when a foetus is generally considered viable.

So, although by default, abortion is a criminal offence, there are sufficient doctors who appreciate that denying a woman an abortion and compelling her to have a child that she doesn't want, is going to be damaging to her physical and mental health. The result is that abortion is pretty much available upon request, and in 2019 a total of 99% of abortions were funded by the NHS.

On the other hand, abortion in the United States, since the *Roe v. Wade* case in 1973, is a protected constitutional *right* under the Fourteenth Amendment of the US Constitution. In coming to their conclusions, the Supreme Court first divided pregnancy into trimesters and ruled that, what a state could do to restrict abortion, would depend on which trimester the pregnancy was in. They ruled that:

- During the first trimester, i.e. weeks 0–13 "the abortion decision and its effectuation must be left to the medical judgement of the pregnant woman's attending physician."
- During the second trimester, i.e. weeks 14–27 "the State, in promoting its interest in the health of the mother, may, **if it chooses**, regulate the abortion procedure in ways that are reasonably related to **maternal health**."
- During the third trimester, i.e. from week 28 "the State in promoting its interest in the **potentiality of human life**… may, **if it chooses**, regulate, and even proscribe, abortion except where it is necessary, in appropriate medical judgement, for the preservation of the **life or health of the mother**."

In effect, a State has no right to interfere with access to abortion during the first trimester. During the second trimester a state can "if it chooses," enact laws designed to protect the health of the mother. Notice, first, that a state is not compelled to enact any laws in this regard and, secondly, that any laws it does enact must relate to maternal health. It is only from week 28 that a state can "if it chooses," enact laws to regulate, or even prohibit, abortion, providing those exceptions are made to protect the life and health of the mother. Again, notice that states are not compelled to enact any laws in this regard, and there are several regions and states that do not put any time limit on when an abortion can be obtained – Alaska, Colorado, Washington D.C., New Hampshire, New Jersey, New Mexico, Oregon and Vermont.

Although it may be fairly obvious when a specific pregnancy puts a woman's life at risk, what does the Court actually mean when it refers to "health"? The *Roe v. Wade* ruling did not define "health", but it was issued on the very same day as another ruling – *Doe v. Bolton* – and in the rulings it was stated that the two were supposed to be read together. In *Doe v. Bolton* we have the following:

> We agree with the District Court, ... that the medical judgment may be exercised in the light of all factors - **physical**, **emotional**, **psychological**, **familial**, and the **woman's age** - relevant to the wellbeing of the patient. All these factors may relate to health.

Anti-abortionists claim that, because "health" is defined so broadly, a State has no power to actually stop a woman getting an abortion which, in effect, allows for abortion on demand, something the Court ruling explicitly rejects. They refer to the following:

> On the basis of elements such as these, appellant and some amici argue that the woman's right is absolute and that she is entitled to terminate her pregnancy at whatever time, in whatever way, and for whatever reason she alone chooses. With this we do not agree.

On the face of it, it would appear that having the right to abortion constitutionally protected would be better than having it criminalized unless two doctors[82] agree with a woman that it will adversely affect her physical or mental health.

However, we need only look at the following passage, by one committed anti-abortionist, to see the problem:

> Intelligent, committed pro-lifers will not be satisfied in principle with anything less than the legal prohibition, or abolition, **of all abortion** (though most pro-lifers are pragmatic enough to accept partial abolitions **as incremental steps toward that goal**). *Peter Kreeft in Three Approaches to Abortion*

Unable to win the abortion argument outright, anti-abortionists in both Great Britain and the United States are trying everything they can to make abortion as difficult as possible for any woman requiring one.

---

[82] The Abortion Act 1967 requires "two registered medical practitioners" to agree that an abortion request meets the necessary conditions.

Probably because abortion in this country is legal solely on health grounds, and not as a matter of *right* as in the US, anti-abortionists have had limited success. For example, since the *Human Fertilisation and Embryology Act 1990* reduced the time limit from 28 weeks to 24 weeks, attempts have been made to reduce it even further. To get an idea of anti-abortionists' tactics we can look at two examples regarding the British politician currently serving as Secretary of State for Digital, Culture, Media and Sport, Nadine Dorries (born 21 May 1957).

On 31 October 2006 she introduced a Private Member's Bill which would have reduced the time limit for abortion from 24 to 21 weeks and introduced a ten-day 'cooling-off' period, during which time the pregnant woman would be required to undergo counselling. Speaking against the bill, Christine McCafferty (born 14 October 1945), pointed out that:

> No new scientific evidence exists to suggest that foetal viability is now 21 weeks. The British Medical Association, the Royal College of Obstetricians and Gynaecologists and the Royal College of Nursing do not believe that there has been sufficient technological improvement to merit a reduction in the current limit. The Nuffield Council on Bioethics has no documented evidence of survival below 24 weeks.

The bill was heavily defeated.

On 7 September 2011, Dorries, along with Labour MP Frank Field, put forward an amendment to the Health and Social Care (Re-committed) Bill, that would have ensured women were offered *independent* abortion counselling. The effect of this amendment, if it were to have been successful, would have stripped abortion providers of their pregnancy counselling roles and opened them up to tenders from, so called, *independent* organisations.

Bids were expected from pregnancy counselling centres run by CareConfidential, which became an independent entity in July 2011 after spinning off from Christian Action Research and Education (CARE). However, BBC's *Newsnight* carried out an investigation into CareConfidential and obtained their training manual *Called to Care*, which contains the following:

> Abortion is undoubtedly a wickedness that grieves God's heart. As we study the Bible we see that life begins within the womb when the human egg is fertilised and then implanted. The deliberate destruction of the developing child at any stage from this point is to deny the life of the human being – a most grievous sin in the eyes of God...

The amendment was, not surprisingly, heavily defeated.

The situation is very different in the US, where the issue has been made far more political. Within two years of the *Roe* decision grassroots organizations opposed to it tried to undermine it with a multitude of legislative regulations. Some 449 of them made it to the floor of state houses, 58 of which became law.

Because the *Roe* decision only gave women the constitutional *right* to an abortion but did not place any obligation on governments to provide it, one line of assault employed was to attack state and federal funding for abortion. The *Hyde Amendment*[83], which was first passed in 1976, placed a ban on the federal funding of abortion unless the pregnancy arose from rape or incest, or the woman's life was in danger.

A major change came in 1992 with the case *Planned Parenthood of Southeastern Pennsylvania v. Casey*, where the Supreme Court upheld four provisions of the *Pennsylvania Abortion Control Act of 1982*. Although the decision in this case confirmed foetal viability as the threshold beyond which the state's interest in protecting foetal life became *compelling* – therefore enabling states to prohibit abortion, providing exceptions were made where the health or life of the pregnant woman was at risk – but it also introduced a different structure of constitutional scrutiny, which required only that state restriction of abortion, prior to foetal viability, did not place an *undue burden* on a woman's right to procreative autonomy through the imposition of a *substantial obstacle* to abortion access.

The only provision the Supreme Court invalidated was that "which commands that, unless certain exceptions apply, a married woman seeking an abortion must sign a statement indicating that she has notified her husband," as it was considered that it placed an *undue burden* on the woman seeking abortion.

---

[83] Named after its original sponsor Henry Hyde (1924–2007).

One of the provisions upheld by the Supreme Court was one which requires that a woman seeking an abortion give her *informed consent* prior to the procedure. This has given states the opportunity to introduce mandatory waiting periods between the counselling session where the consent is given and the actual abortion procedure. Some states require a 72-hour waiting period after in-person counselling, which obviously necessitates two separate appointments.

However, there doesn't appear to be any requirement that the information, given in informed consent consultations, is factual or safe! For example, some states require that the woman be told that *personhood* begins at conception; some inaccurately assert a link between abortion and an increased risk of breast cancer; some require the medically inaccurate information that a medication abortion can be stopped (or reversed) after the woman takes the first dose of pills whereas, according to a Guardian article, dated 27 May 2021, the only high-quality, randomized controlled trial to be conducted on this treatment was halted in 2019 when three women suffered severe haemorrhaging and had to be hospitalized. On the American College of Obstetricians and Gynecologists (ACOG) website[84], we have the following:

> **Facts are important,** especially when discussing the health of women and the American public. Claims regarding abortion "reversal" treatment **are not based**

---

[84] Medication Abortion "Reversal" Is Not Supported by Science | ACOG accessed 13 June 2021.

on science and do not meet clinical standards. The American College of Obstetricians and Gynecologists (ACOG) ranks its recommendations on the strength of the **evidence**, and does not support prescribing progesterone to stop a medical abortion.

Yet, politicians are pushing legislation to require physicians to recite a script that a medication abortion can be "reversed" with doses of progesterone, and to steer women to this care. **Unfounded legislative mandates represent dangerous political interference and compromise patient care and safety.**

To get an idea of the lengths anti-abortionist go to in the US, from 1973, when *Roe* was decided, to 2017, there were 1,193 state level restrictions on abortion! Many of these restrictions are referred to as TRAP[85] laws – exceedingly burdensome licensing requirements, that go well beyond what is required for patient safety; the primary purpose being to limit access to abortion. Most of these TRAP laws apply a state's standards for Ambulatory Surgical Centers (ASCs) to abortion clinics, even though these ASCs provide more invasive, and hence riskier, procedures often using higher levels of sedation. In some cases, TRAP laws are even extended to sites where only medical abortion is administered.

These laws are purported to be for the pregnant woman's health and safety. So how do we know the people behind them are being disingenuous? Let's look at a typical example:

---

[85] Targeted Regulation of Abortion Providers.

The **Texas House Bill 2** was a law that was passed by the 83rd Texas state legislature in 2012. It included four restrictions, two of which were:

- A requirement that all abortion facilities meet the standards of ambulatory surgical centers (ASCs), including facilities that only provide medical abortion.
- A requirement that physicians have admitting privileges at a hospital within 30 miles of the facility.

As mentioned above, standards for ASC's go well beyond what is necessary for abortion clinics, especially those that only provide medical (i.e. nonsurgical) abortion. For example, the minimum corridor width requirement is 8ft, which is to allow for two gurneys[86] to pass each other. Since the law was passed the expense required to meet these excessive and unnecessary requirements has forced many clinics to close in that state, declining from 41 to 19, when this particular restriction was overturned by the Supreme Court in the *Whole Woman's Health v. Hellerstedt* case in 2016.

The requirement that physicians have admitting privileges at a hospital within 30 miles of the facility is a completely unnecessary and irrelevant requirement. Hospitals extend admitting privileges to physicians who admit patients and, thus, provide an income to the hospital. Because abortion is so safe, the risk of needing

---

[86] A gurney is a medical stretcher on wheels.

to transfer a patient from an outpatient abortion clinic to a hospital is virtually negligible, meaning that abortion providers are unlikely to meet the minimum annual patient admissions that some hospitals require. In addition, in the extremely unlikely event that complications did develop, hospitals are obligated, under the federal *Emergency Medical Treatment and Labor Act of 1986*, to provide emergency care, regardless of whether the abortion provider has admitting privileges. Also, because there are now so few abortion clinics, patients have to travel sometimes considerable distances. If they did experience complications within the days following an abortion, they would likely seek treatment from the hospital closest to their home, which would not necessarily be the hospital at which the provider has privileges.

In a *Concurrence* to the *Opinion of the Court*, Justice Ginsburg[87] tellingly wrote:

> The Texas law called H. B. 2 inevitably will reduce the number of clinics and doctors allowed to provide abortion services. Texas argues that H. B. 2's restrictions are constitutional because they protect the health of women who experience complications from abortions. **In truth, "complications from an abortion are both rare and rarely dangerous."** ... Many medical procedures, **including childbirth**, are far more dangerous to patients, yet are not subject to ambulatory-surgical-center or hospital admitting-privileges requirements. ... See also Brief for Social

---

[87] Joan Ruth Bader Ginsburg (1933 – 2020).

Science Researchers 9–11 (comparing statistics on risks for abortion with tonsillectomy, colonoscopy, and in-office dental surgery); ... Given those realities, **it is beyond rational belief that H. B. 2 could genuinely protect the health of women, and certain that the law "would simply make it more difficult for them to obtain abortions."** ... When a State severely limits access to safe and legal procedures, women in desperate circumstances may resort to unlicensed rogue practitioners, faute de mieux, at great risk to their health and safety. ... So long as this Court adheres to Roe v. Wade, ... and Planned Parenthood of Southeastern Pa. v. Casey, ... Targeted Regulation of Abortion Providers laws like H. B. 2 that "do little or nothing for health, but rather strew impediments to abortion," ... cannot survive judicial inspection.

However, with the death of Justice Ginsburg in September 2020, President Donald Trump, an avowedly anti-abortionist, got to nominate his third justice, Amy Coney Barrett (born 1972), following Neil Gorsuch (born 1967) and Brett Kavanaugh (born 1965), to the Supreme Court.

It is telling that, in the Final Presidential Debate on 20 October 2016, between Donald Trump and Hilary Clinton, Trump was asked directly if he wanted the Court to overturn *Roe v. Wade*, and he replied[88]:

Well, if we put another two, or perhaps three, justices on, that's really what's going to... that will happen. And that will happen automatically in my opinion **because I am putting *pro-life* justices on the Court.**

---

[88] https://www.youtube.com/watch?v=Kqbm2YkMP0Q&t=71s

The Supreme Court consists of the Chief Justice of the United States and eight associate justices. The president can nominate anyone to serve on the Court and then, after confirmation of the US Senate, appoints them with a lifetime tenure.

With the appointment of Justice Barrett, there are now six Catholic justices on the Supreme Court, five of whom espouse extremely conservative religious views according to Jamie L. Manson, current president of Catholics for Choice. In a *Guest Essay*, in the New York Times on 27 May 2021, she wrote:

> The [Catholic] hierarchy's influence over its flock has been slipping for decades, which why it has cleverly pivoted to lobbying lawmakers. Catholic organizations have spent years in the Supreme Court making claims to religious liberty that have stripped away U.S. women's rights to free contraceptives, workplace protections and access to health care. **When Catholic leaders flex their considerable policy muscle, their doctrines affect us all, Catholic and non-Catholic. ...**

> Now that the Supreme Court, with its six Catholic justices (five of whom espouse extremely conservative religious views), has decided to take up a case that is a direct challenge to Roe v. Wade, **there has never been a more urgent moment to speak out boldly as people of faith who support the right to access abortion.**

According to the Pew Research Center[89], only 20% of U.S. adults identify as Catholic. That they now comprise

---

[89] https://www.pewforum.org/2019/10/17/in-u-s-decline-of-christianity-continues-at-rapid-pace/

66.7% of the Supreme Court justices, is a probable cause of concern for most Americans!

The case that Manson is referring to is *Dobbs v. Jackson Women's Health Organization*. In March 2018, the state of Mississippi, which currently has one abortion clinic serving a population of approximately three million, spread across 48,432 square miles, passed the *Gestational Age Act*, banning any abortion operation after the first 15 weeks of pregnancy, with exceptions for medical emergencies or severe foetal abnormality, but not including cases of rape or incest.

The clinic sued the state, challenging the constitutionality of the bill. The case was heard by Judge Carlton W. Reeves (born 1964) of the US District Court for the Southern District of Mississippi. In November 2018, Reeves ruled for the clinic and placed an injunction on the state, enjoining them from enforcing the Act. In a sharply worded rebuke, he said that the Mississippi legislature's "professed interest in 'women's health' is pure gaslighting[90]," pointing to evidence of the state's high infant and maternal mortality rates. Calling the law a deliberate attempt by the state to ask the newly conservative-majority Supreme Court to overturn Roe v. Wade, he wrote:

> "The State chose to pass a law **it knew was unconstitutional** to endorse a decades-long campaign,

---

[90] Gaslighting is an insidious form of manipulation and psychological control. Victims of gaslighting are deliberately and systematically fed false information that leads them to question what they know to be true.

fueled by national interest groups, to ask the Supreme Court to overturn Roe v. Wade,"

Commenting further he wrote:

"With the recent changes in the membership of the Supreme Court, it may be that the State believes divine providence covered the Capitol when it passed this legislation. Time will tell."

The state subsequently appealed to the Fifth Circuit, which upheld Reeves' ruling in a 3–0 decision in November 2019. and in June 2020 the state petitioned their appeal of the Fifth Circuit decision to the Supreme Court, which granted *certiorari*[91] to the petition in May 2021.

As it takes at least four justices to agree to hear a case, there appears to be a strong likelihood that a pregnant woman's constitutional *right* to a pre-viable abortion may be overturned. Mary Ziegler, currently the Stearns Weaver Miller Professor of Law at Florida State University College of Law, and one of the leading authorities on the legal history of abortion in America, comments[92]:

… But we can infer from the Court's decision to take this case **that there are at least four justices who think that the Court will uphold this law** and certainly also that there are four justices who think they have a fifth,

---

[91] *Certiorari* is a writ or order by which a higher court reviews a case tried in a lower court.
[92] https://www.youtube.com/watch?v=cED_DMbfKNM

… so there would be no reason for the court to agree to take this case unless those conservatives think they have a majority, **at a minimum to uphold the Mississippi law and perhaps to go much further.**

It will certainly be interesting to see the Courts decision on the case and, if they uphold the *Gestational Age Act*, their reasons for doing so.

Although the above case has nothing to do with the viability of the foetus[93], as both British and U.S. systems currently view this point as having some moral and legal significance, because the foetus can now survive outside the womb, it is worth examining this further.

Anyone claiming that a *human being* is morally significant from the time of conception, will obviously argue that viability is a purely arbitrary point for moral relevancy, and there would certainly appear to be nothing morally significant between a foetus at 24 weeks and one at 23 weeks 6 days. The question is: "Should there be any legal significance?"

Now, a woman doesn't suddenly wake up one morning, after being pregnant for 24 weeks, thinking "Hmm. I'm sure there's something I should have done during the last five months!" Something has happened to cause her to consider abortion after all this time.

For example, consider Sarah, who was a happily married Catholic, and who has been pregnant for

---

[93] No one is arguing that a foetus is viable at 15 weeks.

24 weeks 4 days. She has two beautiful young daughters and a loving husband, Abraham, who had a highly paid job in the city. Sarah, a stay-at-home mum, was quite content with the family she had, but as Abraham had always wanted a son, she had agreed to try one last time. The foetus turned out to be male and the couple were blissfully happy. However, 4 days ago, Abraham was tragically killed in an accident. The sole reason for having a son has now sadly gone and Sarah is left to bring up two young children on her own. After considering the families new circumstances, especially her responsibility to her two daughters, she has decided that having an abortion is her least bad option. Should any legal system we are considering deny her that option?

As the foetus is now considered viable, we could enact a law which either forces her to undergo early induced labour, forces her to undergo a caesarean section, or forces her to carry the foetus to term. Notice that all of these options effectively rob Mary of her moral agency and reduces her to the status of a mere incubator. In Kantian terms she ceases to be seen as "an end" but merely as "a means to an end," something that goes against his categorical imperative!

Whilst examining the issue of abortion from the religious, the ethical, and the legal points of view, it should always be born in mind that, at the heart of the debate, are real women, doing the best they can to cope with the situation they now find themselves in. How we treat them says a lot about the society we are currently living in, who we allow to influence our society, and how we want our society to move forward.

Whilst carrying out research for this book, I came across the Religious Institute[94]. It is a multifaith organization "dedicated to advocating for sexual, gender, and reproductive health, education, and justice in faith communities and society." It has "a network of more than 12,000 religious leaders and people of faith," Considering its religious leanings, I was somewhat surprised to see that its views on abortion were very similar to mine. In *An Open Letter to Religious Leaders on Abortion as a Moral Decision*, issued in 2005, we have the following statements on Scripture and Religious Pluralism:

> **Scripture neither condemns nor prohibits abortion**. It does, however, call us to act compassionately and justly when facing difficult moral decisions. Scriptural commitment to the most marginalized means that pregnancy, childbearing, and abortion should be safe for all women. **Scriptural commitment to truth-telling means women must have accurate information as they make their decisions.**

> No government committed to human rights and democracy can privilege the teachings of one religion over another. No single religious voice can speak for all faith traditions on abortion, nor should government take sides on religious differences. Women must have the right to apply or reject the principles of their own faith without legal restrictions. We oppose any attempt to make specific religious doctrine concerning abortion the law for all Americans or for the women of the world.

---

[94] www.religiousinstitute.org

Particularly interesting from my point of view is that there is no mention of *person* or *personhood* in the letter, but it does include a section *Affirming Women's Moral Agency*:

> We affirm women as **moral agents** who have the **capacity, right** and **responsibility** to make the decision as to whether or not abortion is justified in their specific circumstances. That decision is best made when it includes a well- informed conscience, serious reflection, insights from her faith and values, and consultation with a caring partner, family members, and spiritual counselor.

It is now decision time!

As we saw in Chapter 4, Trent Horn argues that:

> Pro life advocates simply maintain that the state should endorse an answer to the question of when **life begins**, or who counts as a **human being** with a **right to life**, that is backed **by science** and **common sense**.

Well, science does inform us that, from the moment a male's sperm fertilizes a woman's egg, a new *human being* is created. However, what science does not, and cannot, tell us is what moral and legal status that zygote has. We have to work this out for ourselves.

The religious *belief*, that we are comprised of a material body infused with an immortal soul at conception, is as we have seen "not a unanimous tradition" even among Catholics, and one explicitly refuted by many famous religious writers, for example St Anselm:

No human intellect accepts the view that an infant has the rational soul **from the moment of conception.**

In addition, this belief seems inconsistent with belief in an omniscient, omnipotent, and omnibenevolent god, as science now informs us that a majority of fertilized ova spontaneously abort prior to implantation. The *explanation* that "Well, God works in mysterious ways" a stock reply often used by Christians to explain why their prayers have not been answered, is unlikely to *cut the mustard* here. The possibility of twinning up to fourteen days after fertilization also casts considerable doubt on this claim.

As we saw, in the *Introduction*, in contrast to the official Catholic position of trying to make abortion illegal, the Episcopal Church expressed "its unequivocal opposition to any legislative, executive or judicial action on the part of **local, state** or **national** governments that abridges the right of a woman to reach an informed decision about the termination of pregnancy or that would limit the access of a woman to safe means of acting on her decision."

Leaving aside the moral and legal arguments concerning the terms *person* and *personhood*, I think most people, if not all, will agree that any mentally competent adult will satisfy the requirements of a **moral agent,** *viz.* they have the capacity to understand moral arguments and to make decisions based on their own understanding. It, therefore, follows that, in any civilized society, they **must** have the freedom and autonomy to act on those decisions and take responsibility for their actions.

If all mentally competent adults are considered moral agents, then mentally competent pregnant women **must** be included in this category. From this it follows that, if the law cannot, and should not, compel a moral agent to, say, give blood, or donate their bone marrow, even to save the life of another moral agent, then it cannot, and should not, compel a pregnant woman to continue a pregnancy against her will, with all the physical and psychological risks that it would entail.

Further, the unborn, at whatever stage of development, cannot be considered **moral agents**. Neither can babies or young children. Whilst they lack the rational capacities and maturity to direct their own lives without guidance from others, they cannot have the same *rights* as moral agents. However, as members of the species *homo sapiens*, they clearly merit some moral standing and can be classified as **moral patients**. As the progression of human development, from gestation to adulthood, is a continuous and unbroken process, it seems rational to consider that their moral standing increases correspondingly, until eventually they do reach the status of moral agents in their own right.

We saw in the *Introduction* that the World Health Organization reports that "Legal restrictions on abortion do not result in fewer abortions," and that "laws and policies that facilitate access to safe abortion do not increase the rate or number of abortions." One conclusion they draw is that "Restricting legal access to abortion does not decrease the need for abortion, but it is likely to increase the number of women seeking illegal and unsafe abortions, leading to increased morbidity and mortality."

Since 2015 there has been an International Safe Abortion Day on 28 September each year. In 2018, speaking the day before "a group of United Nations human rights experts urged governments across the world to **decriminalise** abortion and enhance their progress towards ensuring the right of every woman or girl to make autonomous decisions about her pregnancy." They assert that[95]:

> The singling out of abortion, as a medical procedure, for criminalization has contributed to its stigmatization and women being targeted for it. **The idea that abortion is blameworthy is a cultural construction. The fact is that it should be a safe medical procedure that women and girls should have access to when they need it.** ...

> Legal frameworks for abortion have typically been designed to **control women's decision-making** through the use of criminal law. Many legal frameworks generally prohibit abortion and make it legal only on specific grounds **that do not capture the range of circumstances in which women and girls may need abortions.** Moreover, strict time limits for abortion often cause women to be in situations where their abortions become illegal. These legal restrictions frequently converge with the practical barriers to effectively deny abortion to pregnant women and girls at the expense of their dignity and well-being. ...

> Denying women access to services, **which only they require,** and failing to address their specific

---

[95] See: https://www.ohchr.org/EN/NewsEvents/Pages/Display News.aspx?NewsID=23644&LangID=E. Accessed 22/06/ 2021.

reproductive health needs, **is inherently discriminatory.** Gender-based discrimination in the administration of medical services **violates women's human rights and dignity.**

For those arguing about *human rights* for the unborn, they point out that:

> It was **well established** in the 1948 Universal Declaration of Human Rights and upheld in the International Covenant on Civil and Political Rights that **international human rights are conferred to those who have been born.** But some propagate a dangerous rhetoric that the rights of a pregnant woman and fetal interests must be equally protected. **However, there is no such assertion in international human rights law.**

And they should know! They go on to say:

> Unsafe abortion is among the leading causes of death for pregnant women. Restrictive abortion laws endanger lives of women and imposes hardship on them, therefore the claim often made by opponents of abortion that their stance is "pro-life" is misleading.

International organizations are not the only ones calling for the decriminalization of abortion. In a document entitled *RCOG and FSRH key messages on safe abortion*, the Royal College of Obstetricians & Gynaecologists, along with *The Faculty of Sexual & Reproductive Healthcare*, made these points:

> Safe abortion is essential healthcare and a **human right.** ...

Not only is safe abortion essential healthcare, the RCOG and FSRH considers women and girls' ability to determine their own sexual and reproductive health a key principle for ensuring the human rights of all. **Denying pregnant people safe abortion care may lead to violations of their right to life, their right to health, their right to privacy and can in some cases amount to cruel, inhumane or degrading treatment. ...**

Safe abortions are an essential part of sexual and reproductive health; they should be an integrated component of sexual and reproductive healthcare and be available as part of routine health services. Abortions can be safely provided by healthcare professionals such as midwifes and nurses and should be safe, **legal**, high quality and accessible (i.e. affordable and local). **Safe abortion care should be guaranteed as part of a human rights-based framework to health. ...**

Making abortion illegal does not stop pregnant people from seeking abortions, but it does result in them obtaining abortions that are potentially unsafe, putting them at risk of complications, disability and death. **To save lives, abortion should not be subject to criminal sanctions for patients, healthcare professionals and others who are assisting in accessing abortion care.** It should be subject to regulatory and professional standards, in line with other medical procedures, placing sexual and reproductive health, rights and autonomy at the heart of abortion regulations. **There should be no legal time limit for abortions that are performed to safeguard the health and safety of pregnant people, women and girls. ...**

Decriminalising abortion is also key to reducing stigma experienced by both providers and those seeking abortions.

Although, for the time being at least, abortion is still a constitutionally protected *right* in the United States, we have seen how anti-abortionist have worked hard to make it as difficult as possible to access. It is, therefore, worth including these statements from the *Abortion Policy* of the American College of Obstetricians and Gynecologists' (ACOG), which was reaffirmed as recently as November 2020:

> Induced abortion is an essential component of women's health care. Like all medical matters, decisions regarding abortion should be made by patients in consultation with their health care providers **and without undue interference by outside parties. Like all patients, women obtaining abortion are entitled to privacy, dignity, respect, and support. ...**
>
> ACOG is opposed to laws and regulations that operate to prevent advancements in medicine. For example, laws that prohibit health care providers from following current evidence-based protocols for medical abortion disregard scientific progress and prevent providers from offering patients the best available care. Likewise, the state and federal laws that prohibit specific surgical abortion procedures disrupt the evolution of surgical technique and prevent physicians from providing the best or most appropriate care for some patients.

When I set out to investigate the abortion *issue*, I already knew that some of the things some Christians claimed were, to say the least, unsubstantiated and disingenuous. I was not clear, however, on how abortion *squared* with the *rights* of the unborn. I am now sure that abortion should be a private matter between the pregnant woman and her physician. It should, therefore, be decriminalized, with easy access to advice and facilities being available to all women that need them.

If, after considering all of the information contained in this book, you disagree with my conclusion then, as a moral agent, you are perfectly entitled to do so. Just remember that pregnant women are moral agents also, and as such their decisions, just like yours, should be respected.

Lightning Source UK Ltd.
Milton Keynes UK
UKHW050116290422
402188UK00006B/115